Rowing

To my parents, with gratitude

Wolfgang Fritsch

Rowing

Training – Fitness – Leisure

Meyer & Meyer Sport

Original title:
Fritsch, Wolfgang: Handbuch für den Rudersport
Training – Kondition – Freizeit
3., überarb. Neuauflage. – Aachen : Meyer und Meyer, 1999
Translated by Robert McMurray

British Library Cataloguing in Publication Data
A catalogue record for this book is available from the British Library

Fritsch, Wolfgang:
Rowing: Training – Fitness – Leisure / Wolfgang Fritsch.
[Transl.: Robert McMurray].
– Oxford: Meyer & Meyer Sport (UK) Ltd., 2000
ISBN 1-84126-024-X

©2000 by Meyer & Meyer Sport (UK) Ltd.
Oxford, Aachen, Olten (CH), Vienna, Quebec, Lansing/Michigan,
Adelaide, Auckland, Johannesburg, Budapest
Member of the World
Sportpublishers' Association
Cover photo: Bongarts Sportpressefoto, Hamburg
Photos on pages 12, 86 (upper), 93 (lower), 97, 98, 150 and 157 were made
available with the kind permission of Ekkehard Braun.
Cover design: Birgit Engelen, Stolberg
Cover and type exposure: frw, Reiner Wahlen, Aachen
Editorial: Dr. Irmgard Jaeger, Aachen, John Coghlan, Paul Castle
Printed and bound in Germany
by Druckpunkt Offset, Bergheim
ISBN 1-84126-024-X
e-mail: verlag@meyer-meyer-sports.com

Contents

Preface to the Third Edition

Dr Fritsch designed his book on "Rowing" for long-term use. There has been a major demand for the book since its first appearance in 1988. The time has now come for a new edition.

Rowing training and instruction must increasingly respond to the needs of adults, because, happily, young people are not the only newcomers to rowing.

More than ever before, top athletes as well as less senior competitors and recreational rowers want to train according to the latest theories. The last decade has seen a number of changes in boat design and materials technology.

In an increasingly varied sport such as rowing it is fortunate that this book sets a written standard. Not everyone will want to closely follow it, but the information in it will always be available as a standard of comparison. In this context the importance of this book for the German Rowing Association as well as the amount of work put into it has certainly increased.

It is fortunate that the author, Dr. Fritsch, has been a member of the Managing Committee of the German Rowing Association for many years. He not only successfully headed the Science and Training Committee but also gives encouragement to other spheres, thus ensuring that fields such as rowing areas and the environment are taken into consideration.

Our thanks and recognition to Dr. Fritsch.

Professor Dr. Wolfgang Maennig

Chairman of the German Rowing Association

Preface to the First and Second Editions

An experienced sports scientist and successful coach has presented us with a book which is both an atlas and a signpost.

The book is a successful combination of theory and practice. As a systematic overview of rowing it is a welcome aid for beginners, coaches, those in training and in clubs, in short, for all those interested in rowing. In addition to the basics, the author has also included important contributions to current topics such as rowing and the environment. He also gives tips on the numerous and varied opportunities for social activities in a rowing club based on fitness and well-being, upon which many people place much importance.

The author's own aim of using this book to awaken an interest in rowing in many people supports the efforts of the German Rowing Association in helping as many people as possible to understand and appreciate the special characteristics and advantages of this unique sport.

For this Dr. Wolfgang Fritsch deserves the special thanks of the German Rowing Association.

Henrik Lotz
Honorary Chairman of the German Rowing Association
Chairman of the German Rowing Association 1983-1995

Dedication

No branch of sport can do without a constant scrutiny of its content, basic principles and methods. New knowledge, increasing demands, a constantly changing conception of sport, as well as new standards for the sport and what it offers force us to constantly rethink it.

This new book by Wolfgang Fritsch answers these questions. Based on proven knowledge and experience, the book gives well-illustrated information on learning to row, training and competing as well as rowing for pleasure.

An essential part of this book is the remarks on methods and rowing techniques.

As a former head of the Science and Education Committee of the German Rowing Association I am especially pleased about this successful application of scientific knowledge, all the more so because this book offers special assistance in the teaching of newcomers to the sport. This book makes learning and coaching of rowing easy.

The book depicts rowing as a sport which derives its importance from experiences in nature, social life, performance and competition as well as enjoyable excursions.

This book is a must for coaches, trainers and rowing teachers. It offers both encouragement and help to everyone connected with our sport in schools, institutes of higher education and clubs.

Friedhelm Kreiß

Honorary Member of the German Rowing Association

Why take-up rowing?

1. Introduction

Rowing is an exciting, multi-faceted sport which can be learned at any age. This rowing manual seeks to awaken interest and enthusiasm in those readers wishing to find out about the sport and what it has to offer. For those who have already decided to take up rowing, it provides a systematic overview of the essential conditions under which the sport is carried out. It is thus intended for beginners, coaches, club officials and up-and-coming competitive rowers. It describes the opportunities rowing offers, but also points out the obligations on the part of rowing clubs and their officials to do justice to the variety and opportunities of this sport.

Rowing is not a sport with a large number of participants and will not become a mass sport in the foreseeable future. Nevertheless this does not mean that a wide section of the public should not be made aware of the special aspects and advantages of this unique sport. The primary goals of a rowing association and its member-clubs must be to retain their members and to improve the quality of the sport they offer. Some progress has already been made in this area but there is still a lot more to be done.

Rowing does not compete with the so-called prestige sports like riding, golfing, sailing, skiing, and tennis. Rowing's reputation compared to other sports consists of the combination of several points: it is closely connected with nature and the environment, it combines a variety of associated ideas and a host of different social experiences and presents an exceptional form of education.

Rowing has also succeeded in distancing itself from specific developments seen in other sports such as commercialisation, manipulation of performance, etc. Furthermore, rowing's reputation is marked by competition and achievement. Rowers are often regarded as being *strong* and *fit*.

About the Third Edition

Developments in rowing continue apace. Since the first and, shortly thereafter, the second edition of this book, there have been many changes requiring a few amendments. The third edition is an attempt to keep up with these developments. Thus – apart from a modern presentation/layout (graphics, photos, tables, etc.) – some chapters have been revised, completed and corrected. I owe a special word of thanks to the Meyer & Meyer Publishing Company for its professional advice and cooperation.

2. What Does Rowing Have to Offer?

Rowing is Both a Team as well as an Individual Sport

Rowing is a team sport which differs from many other team sports such as football or hockey. In all types of team sports the individual's performance must be coordinated with that of another team member. While this takes place in the form of cooperation in field sports – quite different activities are partially coordinated with each other – in rowing all team members must act together or "co-act" within a certain time frame. Tradition and rowing's historical development in competitive team structure has resulted in "formed" pairs, fours and eights (each with a cox and without), as well as the single sculls as an opportunity to present individual performance or for practice.

A rowing eight – the epitome of a sports team

Rowing Is a Healthy Sport Which Offers Fitness and Good Physical Condition

As an endurance sport rowing offers an outstanding opportunity to counter the widespread effects of sedentary life and other side-effects of modern civilisation. It also offers the opportunity for people of all ages to keep fit. In contrast to many other sports, rowers are rarely injury-prone and can perform their sport all year round. Unlike most other sports rowing uses a wide range of muscle groups. Through the combination of strength and endurance, almost all physical performance factors are increased without resorting to additional sports, equipment and other measures.

Rowing Is an Outdoor Sport and Outdoor Experience

If one ignores training equipment designed to simulate the strain and movement of oars, rowing must be carried out outdoors. The description "outdoor sport" is especially important, since the number of sports that can be carried out indoors, and those outdoor sports using exterior forms of energy (motors, wind), are increasing. Navigating unknown rivers and lakes, visiting overseas regattas in unfamiliar countries, observing nature and animal life from an unfamiliar perspective, or spending days or weeks in a tent, away from home, offers the young and old a special experience and adventure.

Rowing Is Inexpensive

The boats and oars are supplied by the club. If one compares the membership fees with those of other sports clubs with similar equipment costs, rowing clubs are much cheaper. With regular maintenance, everyday rowing equipment lasts much longer.

People of all Ages Can Row; Rowing Is an Educational Sport

As opposed to many other sports, old and young, men and women, parents and children and the handicapped and non-handicapped alike can participate in this sport together. Through relatively simple and easy-to-learn movements, the demands on mainly aerobic endurance and relatively *self-contained* forms of exercise homogenous and heterogenous groups can be formed.

Especially in the Anglo-Saxon countries rowing has a great tradition as a school sport. Countless school rowing teams bear witness to the fact that rowing as a team sport presents an opportunity for social contact and furthering one's own interests. The special structure of this team sport provides an educationally useful social experience.

Rowing Is a Club Sport

Rowing is mainly carried out in clubs, which, apart from fulfilling their members' wishes to go rowing, can also satisfy a number of other needs. They offer an opportunity for social contact amongst sport hobbyists thereby acting as a means and an end for the sports-oriented person to share one's interests. Apart from the organisational opportunities and conditions for the carrying out of this sport, clubs have an immense repertoire of both formal and informal forms of social involvement and communication, such as social activities, group life, friendship and parties, etc. and can offer both young and old a second home.

Rowing requires intensive training.

Rowing Is a Competitive and High-Performance Sport

A comprehensive competition programme – from childhood (from about eleven years) to advanced old age – offers ample opportunity for those who want to try their strength in organised competition. In Germany there are up to 100 regattas between spring and autumn. These allow comparisons at all levels and classes of competition. Rowing as a competitive and performance sport has always been very attractive. The great effort needed for training and the enormous work load require total commitment from the athletes.

Rowing Is a Sport for the Disabled

Rowing is easy to learn, and through their participation physically handicapped people, especially the blind, become equal partners. The danger of isolation, loss of social contact and the development of an inferiority complex, which the handicapped acquire rapidly, is reduced by the special opportunities offered by rowing. Countless activities, projects and groups in the German Rowing Association bear witness to these opportunities.

Getting ready for a day on the water.

Rowing Is a Leisure and Family Sport

Leisure sport is generally characterised as the opportunity to take up a sport in groups of the same age, sex and ability. At the same time, however, the special interests and abilities of the participants are taken into account through rule changes in practices, games and competitions. Rowing offers excellent opportunities for unwinding, getting together socially and having fun with family and friends. The knowledge that one can do as one likes without having to perform to a set standard or norm is considered to be a way of extending one's horizons for leisure rowers, both as individuals and in family groups.

The above opportunities can certainly be expanded upon in one way or another. Rowing offers both opportunities and obligations: for sports hobbyists it is an opportunity to make use of the many facets of rowing or to gain special experience in one area or another of the sport; for rowing clubs and rowing associations it is an opportunity to publicise rowing, thereby making it better known and improving its image.

More and more clubs in the German Rowing Association are fulfilling their obligations with what they have to offer and, with qualified coaches, are enriching the whole sport.

3. How This Book Is Laid Out

This book is meant as an introduction to rowing and is designed to present the broad band of what rowing has to offer. A broad and general spectrum is developed from the abundance of material, but in individual areas, overspecific hints are avoided.

Part 1 contains a section on the *fundamentals* of rowing which explains the equipment and how the sport is learned.

Part 2 is concerned with oar movement (*technique*) and the development of the physical requirements of rowing (*training*). Special emphasis is placed on practical examples of how techniques are taught as well as ways to improve physical ability.

Part 3 describes various areas of application available in a rowing club:
- Rowing as a means of obtaining *fitness* and *health*.
- Rowing as a form of *recreation*.
- *Basic Training* in order to ensure new recruits to rowing.

Questions and problems about high-performance rowing have been omitted from this book. The chapters on technique and training in Part 2 should therefore be applied to all areas of experience.

Finally, the appendix gives tips on further reading, information on the most important competition rules and awards.

Eights just after the start

PART 1: THE FUNDAMENTALS

The Rower's Equipment

1. Types of Boats

The many types of boats reflect the tradition and the technical development of rowing in special ways. Two types of boats have basically developed which are used in very different ways in leisure rowing and in competitive sport:

1. The "tub" more or less means "a light dinghy" and is used mostly for teaching and training as well as recreational rowing. As a rule it is stable and is less sensitive to exterior influences and mistakes made by occupants.

2. The racing boat, on the other hand, is of very light construction; in training and competition it is adjusted a lot more to the characteristics and abilities of the rowers, necessitating very expensive construction.

The essential feature distinguishing these two types of boats – apart from the weight – and hence the use of more or less expensive materials in the construction, is the shape. Tubs are wider and their shape and weight are subject to certain regulations (see table 1), while racing boats have only been subject to minimum weights in the last few years.

The tub also has an outer keel, a continuous gunwale and a gunwale slit. The racing boat has no outer keel, only a partial inner keel, a lowered splash board and two canvasses (see figures 1 & 2). The high demands on load-bearing capacity, strength and stability were made possible up until only a few years ago, mainly through the use of wood in the building of boats.

Cedar or plywood was used for the shell, and spruce, ash or beech for the interior. Since then, however, manufacturers have relied heavily on the use of plastics, e.g. fibreglass-reinforced polyester resin.

The Tub

Within the tub boat type one usually distinguishes between A-, B-, C-, D- and, recently, E-boats. In the last few years boats made of artificial fibres have caught on increasingly, and recently – as far as new orders are concerned, at least – represent the greater proportion of all boats used.

	A-tub	B-tub	C-tub	D-tub	E-tub
Material	wood	wood	wood	wood	plastic
Method of construction	clinker	clinker	plastic	plastic	with wood
(Width/Length) Weight: Wood/Plastic					
Single scull (with cox: very unusual) Double scull			0.78 m wide 7 m long		
Double scull / Coxed pair (with cox: fairly unusual)					
Triple scull (unusual)	0.9 m 8.25 m 85 kg	0.78 m 8.5 m 75 kg	0.78 m 8.5 m 60 kg / 85 kg	0.9 m 8.5 m 70 kg / 90 kg	
Coxed four (also called a "quad")					
Coxed quad Quintuple scull (fairly rare)	1 m / 10.5 m 110 kg	0.78 m / 11 m 100 kg	0.78 m / 11 m 85 kg / 110 kg	1 m / 11 m 90 kg / 120 kg	0.9 m / 11 m 80 kg / 90 kg
Eight		0.85 m/ 17.5 m 185 kg	0.85 m/ 17.5 m 150 kg		

Table 1: Dimensions of the tubs

Of the tubs, the C-boat is the clear choice, making up between some 2/3 to 3/4 of tubs built. Of the new boats the E-tub is also gaining popularity.

A- and B-boats are so-called "clinker-boats" with roof-tile-like planks laid over one another and are made mostly of cedar or mahogony. Because of their greater weight and higher production costs, they are built only rarely.

C-, D- and E-boats have a smooth exterior surface made of glued plywood or of plastic, e.g. fibreglass-reinforced polyester resin.

C-tub	Coxed pair	Coxed four	Eight
Overall length	8.5 m	11 m	17.5 m
Maximum width	0.78 m	0.78 m	0.85 m
Width at waterline	0.65 m	0.65 m	0.7 m
Minimum depth	0.32 m	0.33 m	0.32 m
Minimum weight	60 kg	80 kg	150 kg

Table 2: Prescribed measurements for C-tubs

The Racing Boat

In competitive rowing the dimensions of the boats are the result of experience, so they differ only in minor details.

There are no compulsory rules for racing boats except a minimum weight requirement which must be compensated for if the boat falls short of this.

Sculling boats	Approx. width (at waterline)	Approx. length (overall)	Minimum weight*
(Single scull)	0.27 – 0.29 m	7.8 – 8.3 m	14 kg
Double scull	0.33 – 0.35 m	9.4 – 10 m	27 kg
Quad	0.43 – 0.46 m	11.8 – 12.9 m	52 kg
Rowing boats			
(Coxless) pair	0.33 – 0.36 m	9.4 – 10 m	27 kg
(Coxed) pair	0.37 m	10 m	32 kg
Coxless four	0.43 – 0.46 m	11.8 – 12.9 m	50 kg
Coxed quad	0.46 – 0.47 m	12.9 – 13.65 m	51 kg
Eight (must be sectionable)	0.55 – 0.57 m	16.85 – 17.8 m	96 kg

Table 3: Dimensions for racing boats (*according to FISA-regulations)

At regattas three construction types may be found:

1. Boats glued together out of *solid wood* with wooden interior fittings are becoming less and less common at regattas. An increasingly rarely practised method is to stretch a thin 2-3 mm wooden veneer over the boat's ready-made load-bearing framework.

2. With the *composite method* the boat's shell is made out of fibreglass, reinforced plastic or kevlar, with the interior fittings made out of wood.

3. Increasing use is being made of all *plastic boats*, especially in championship rowing. Some are up to 10% lighter than other boats and are made of carbon and epoxy resin. In addition, the keel, the wooden strip at the bow-end of the gunwales and the inner reinforcing ribs are reinforced with extremely strong materials such as carbon and kevlar.

A rowboat in a lock.

Special Types of Boats

Even rarer are *sea-gigs* and *tubs*. Used initially for newcomers to rowing, they now offer a special experience, e.g. for recreational rowing or rowing on very choppy water.

Sea-gigs are similar to normal gigs with the slide on the gunwale. Because they have no riggers, these crafts are even wider (1–1.2 m) than gigs and the rowers' seats are arranged on one side of the boat then the other alternatively.

Tubs are so wide that each pair of adjacent rowers' positions can even be separated by a walkway. They are over 10 m long and can weigh between 400–800 kg (see photo on p. 25 above).

For training, but especially for rowing in general, rowers like to use plastic sculls and doubles as well. They are shaped like a racing boat but are built more strongly and are somewhat more heavy than racing boats.

The plastics used here are not as high in quality or expensive as those used in modern racing boat construction, which gives these plastic boats used for ordinary rowing an built-in advantage.

Some plastic boats are produced as special versions for children (*junior boats*) and are adjusted for girls' and boys' different body sizes and weights. For childrens' regattas, for example, only those plastic boats not exceeding 7.4 m in length and weighing a minimum of 18 kg are permitted.

Boat type	Approx. width (at waterline)	Approx. length (overall)
Junior scull	0.27 m	7.35 m
Scull / racing scull	0.29 m	8.35 m
Single C-scull	0.58 m	7 m
"Trimmy"	0.75 m	5.5 m
Junior coxed pair	0.35 m	9 m
Coxed pair / coxed racing pair	0.36 m	9.9 m

Table 4: An overview of training boats

2. The Parts of a Boat (Illustrations 1–3)

1	Gate	9	Sliding seat	a	Thwartship distance
2	Rigger	10	Slide	b	Height of gate or rigger
3	Gate-pin	11	Inwhale	d	Gate take-off board
4	Cross-rib	12	Cox's seat	bb	Port side
5	Saxboard	13	Rudder	stb	Starboard side
6	Stretcher	14	Rigger brace	A	Bow
7	Footplate	15	Canvas	B	Stern
8	Interior keel	16	Fin	1-4	Rowers' seats

3. Categories of Boats

Boats basically carry one, two, four or eight rowers. Some boats may also carry a coxswain. The boats are powered by oars (one for every team member) or sculls (two smaller oars per rower).

The one-man boat (or skiff) is always a scull, whereas the eight as a rule is powered by larger oars and has a coxswain. The fact that there is a given number of different types of tubs and racing boats is a result of the historic development of rowing and has no compelling logic. That means, for example, that the "coxed six" no longer exists; for tubs, on the other hand, we occasionally see some clubs with a "coxed scull", a double three (as a convertible double with cox) and also a double eight.

Eight types of competition boats have been developed, which are used as international types, e.g. in World Championships (see table 5).

There are also World Championships for lightweights and juniors of both sexes. Both the World Championships and the Olympics went through repeated changes in the early days; nowadays they adapt to the developments in competitive rowing and the representation of individual classes.

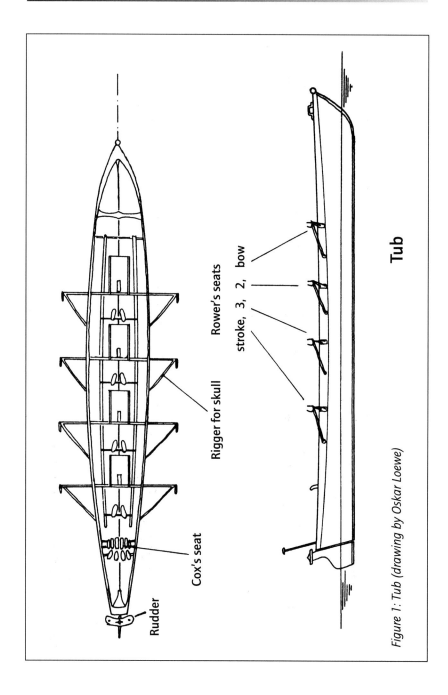

Rower's seats

stroke, 3, 2, bow

Rigger for skull

Cox's seat

Rudder

Tub

Figure 1: Tub (drawing by Oskar Loewe)

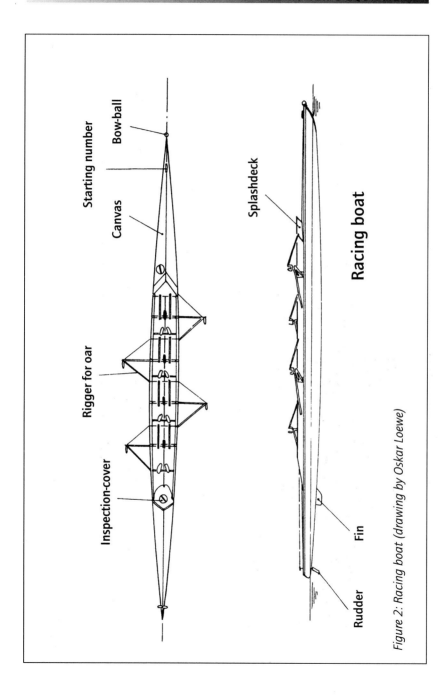

Figure 2: Racing boat (drawing by Oskar Loewe)

The parts of the boat

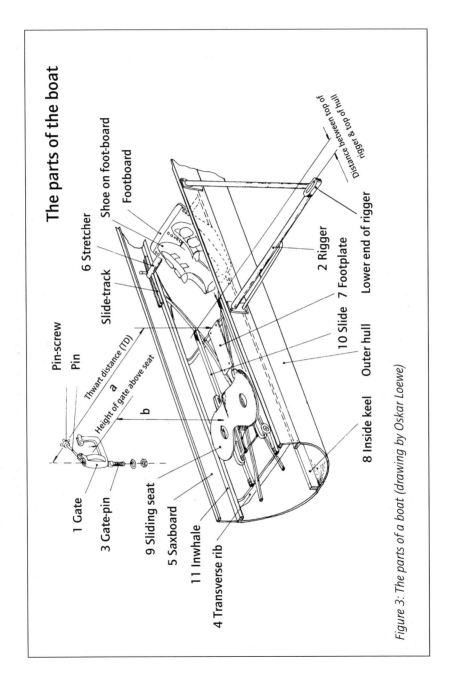

1 Gate
3 Gate-pin
9 Sliding seat
5 Saxboard
11 Inwhale
4 Transverse rib

Pin-screw
Pin

6 Stretcher

Slide-track

Shoe on foot-board

Footboard

Thwart distance (TD)

a

Height of gate above seat

b

2 Rigger
7 Footplate

Lower end of rigger

10 Slide

8 Inside keel   Outer hull

Distance between top of
rigger & top of hull

Figure 3: The parts of a boat (drawing by Oskar Loewe)

Type of Boat	Example	Men	Women	Mens' Lightweight	Womens' Lightweight	Junior Mens'	Junior Womens'
Single scull		◆/X	◆/X	◆	◆	◆	◆
Double scull		◆/X	◆/X	◆/X	◆/X	◆	◆
Quad		◆/X	◆/X	◆	◆	◆	◆
Coxless pair		◆/X	◆/X	◆	◆	◆	◆
Coxed pair		◆				◆	
Coxless four		◆/X	◆	◆/X		◆	◆
Coxed four		◆	◆			◆	
Coxed eight		◆/X	◆/X	◆		◆	◆

Table 5: Types of boats and the categories in which they are used for the Olympic Games (X) and the World Championships (◆) (current status until the Olympic Games in 2000)

4. The Oars

Development in oar production (long as well as short) was similar to that of boats. In competitive rowing only oars made of synthetic materials are used. For teaching purposes, recreational and everyday rowing, less expensive wooden oars are adequate. Traditional wooden oars, produced from fir or spruce, are built by hand with a hollow shaft or stock in order to take the pressure and the tension on each side of the shaft. As a rule a wedge is fitted under the sleeve, guaranteeing a 4° angle and which, like the reinforcing on the rear side of the shaft, is made of ash.

A normal wooden oar weighs about 4 kg; a longer one about 2.5 kg. The high-quality plastic oars are quite a bit lighter and can be made in varying degrees of hardness, to adjustable lengths and with blades of varying shapes. The negligible fatigue of plastic as opposed to wood, combined with a greater resistance to blows and scratches, make for a longer life and more intense use in competitive rowing.

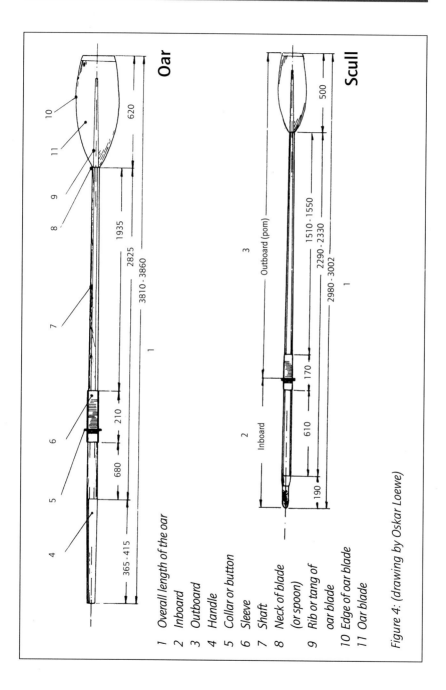

1 Overall length of the oar
2 Inboard
3 Outboard
4 Handle
5 Collar or button
6 Sleeve
7 Shaft
8 Neck of blade
   (or spoon)
9 Rib or tang of
   oar blade
10 Edge of oar blade
11 Oar blade

Figure 4: (drawing by Oskar Loewe)

5. Rigging a Boat

In rowing, "rigging" a boat means suiting and adjusting the equipment (boat and oars) to each rower's physique and level of physical fitness as well as the specific uses it will be put to.

Proper training for the newcomer to rowing, making use of the strength of a top rower or the economical work in recreational rowing is only possible if the boat is properly rigged. In the course of the development of boats and oars, certain uses have emerged which must be taken into consideration in the construction of a boat.

For this reason the average body weight of the rower the boat is to be built for should be taken into consideration when ordering. The average height of the gate, maximum and minimum thwartship distance, as well as the position of the gate in relation to the main transverse should also be borne in mind. Special features like the length of the slide for the seat, the sliding seat, shoe-size (if possible); the adjustment of the cox's shoe on the port or starboard side and the type of gate must also be supplied to the boatbuilder.

The essential step when getting a boat ready for the water is to establish what sort of use the boat or oars will be put to. Will they be used to teach adult beginners for recreational rowing, or as a tub in competitions in a rowing-training programme for young people in German schools?

Certainly, the rowing club may be obliged to use one boat from several groups for various types of rowing, but it is helpful to determine the areas in which the boat will be used – at least in order to adjust it for various uses.

While it must be borne in mind that boats can be bought with settings that can be adjusted to the individual rower(s), it also means that – and this is important for racing boats – they are heavier, more susceptible to damage and do not last as long.

All clubs should check the settings on their boats regularly and adjust them according to the use they will be put to. Incorrect settings lead to rowing errors and can cause strain or injury.

	Everyday rowing	Recreational rowing	Children/ Learners	Competition rowing	Necessary settings or adjustments	Tools required
Gate						
Gate height	X	X	X	X	Hole for rigger, washers	Tool for measuring height, surveyor's pole, spirit level
Thwartship distance	–	–	X	X	Moving the gate-pin on the rigger	Tape measure
Gate	–	–	–	X	Perpendicular adjustment	Plumbine, spirit level, pitch gauge
Angle of construction	–	–	X	X	Turn excentric inset & wedges	Pitch gauge; spirit level
Slide						
Longitudinal direction	–	–	X	X	Length of slide, lengthways adjustment	Tape measure
Stretcher						
Longitudinal direction	X	X	X	X	Move in the direction of the boat	
Angle of footboard	–	–	–	X	Alter the angle	Protractor if necessary
Height of footboard	X	X	X	X	Set the rowing shoes/ heel caps higher/lower	
Oars						
Inset	–	–	–	–	Fit a new sleeve	Pitch gauge
Oar-length	–	–	–	X	Lengthen/shorten the oar	Tape measure
Angle of leverage	X	X	X	X	Adjust the ring-clamps	Tape measure
Blade-shape	–	–	–	–	Change the blades	
Rudder						
Shape	–	–	–	X	Changing the rudder	
Footrudder (portside or starboard)	–	X	–	X	Adjust the rudder-line, change the shoe	

Table 6: Rigging the boat

One useful way of rigging a boat is the following:

1. Establish what the boat and oars will be used for.
2. Establish who will be using the boat (e.g. the rower's average weight and height).
3. Screw on the rigger (establish the average height of the gate-pin).
4. Put the boat on an even keel and screw the rigger on tight.
5. Check to see that the gate is perpendicular.
6. Measure the height of the gate from the side of the hull or the seat; adjust the height of the gate.
7. Adjust the distance of the gate-pin or the slide in the direction of the length of the boat.
8. Adjust the distance of the gate from the centre of the boat.
9. Adjust the angle of the gate-pin (measure this with the gate and the oar-blade).
10. Make sure all screws are tight.

Necessary Tools and Accessories:

- Spanner: 10/11, 13/14, 17/19
- Screwdrivers (various sizes)
- Spirit level, rule, yard stick, plumbline
- Height-gauge or surveyor's pole
- Two screw-clamps and two cross-bars
- Accessories: spare screws, nuts, slotted insets, building wedges, protractors.

Stretcher

This part must be sufficiently adjustable for all boats, since this is the most important adjustment of the rower to the boat and vice-versa. The way the stretcher is adjusted affects and compensates for the body-size, dimensions of the handle, the angle of the oars, the power transfer, and not least rowing technique.

All boats should be adjustable in length and according to the height of the rower's heels. In competitive rowing an adjustable angle is also recommended, i.e. the angle of the foot-board to the horizontal plane (as a rule about 40°–45°). Special shoes which are fixed to the stretcher are helpful when rowing, as these offer better stability.

Adjustments of the stretcher can have the following effects:

- The further the stretcher is set towards the stern, the greater is the forward reach, the less the backward lean, the less the seat travel and the less room at the finish.

- The further the stretcher is set in the direction of the bow, the smaller is the angle of the backward lean, the more room is available for lifting one's body out of the boat; and the rower may have problems putting his legs down flat.

- The higher the heel-cap of the shoe at the stretcher is, the more difficult it is for the rower to come into the backward lean and the more the rower has to bend his legs in order to take up this position.

- The lower the heels and the less the legs push horizontally, the more easily the rower can assume the forward reach and the more his thighs knock against the crossrib.

- The steeper the stretcher is, the more effective the final pull on the oars, the less contact the heels have with the base of the stretcher and the more difficult it is to take up the forward lean.

- The flatter the base of the stretcher is, the more comfortable the rower is in the forward lean and the more his feet are overstretched in the backward lean.

Sliding Seat and Slide-path

The slide-path consists of two rails, 16.5 cm, 23 cm or 28 cm wide, depending on the width of the boat. It rises at the bow-end by about 1.5 cm and is set at between 2–8 cm towards the stern of a racing boat, and about 0.3 cm behind the gate towards the stern on training and recreational boats. This setting influences the rower's position during the first part of the pull on the oar, and the use of the slide-path is determined by the setting of the stretcher.

Rigger and Gate

From the construction of the rigger – steel, aluminium or plastic, depending on what a particular boat is to be used for – a high degree of resistance to, and the ability to recover from strain, along with low weight is expected. If desired, the boatyard can supply riggers on which the height can be progressively adjusted and on which the distance between each gate can be altered. However, the latter is recomended only for training and competition purposes, while height adjustment is necessary for all boats.

The extreme strain on the gate is taken up by a steel gate-pin sticking vertically out of the top of the rigger into which the plastic gates are inserted and fixed in place. Apart from the height adjustment on the rigger (in cm), a finer adjustment by use of washers on the gate should also be possible for racing boats. Essentially, the height of the gate, the angle of the rigger, and the distance between the top of the gate and the stretcher are adjustable.

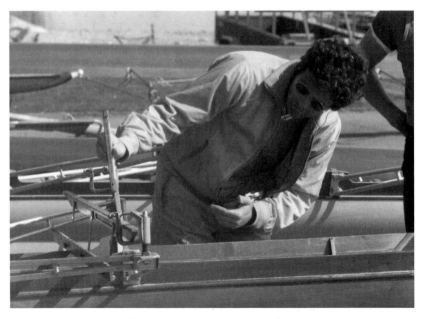

Measuring the height of the gate

The Height of the Gate and the Distance between the Top of the Gate and the Stretcher

- The higher the gate (above the lowest point of the sliding seat), the greater the freedom of hand movement and the more unstable the boat becomes.

- The lower the gate, the more stable the boat and the less latitude there is for the rower's hand movements during and between each stroke.

- The greater the distance between the top of the gate and the stretcher, the greater the momentum, the less force can be exercised on the oar, the less leverage there is during boating and the greater the strain on the rigger.

- The less distance between the gates, the higher the pressure appears to be, and the greater is the angle of effort.

The Angle of the Gate

In competitive rowing especially it is necessary for the angle of the area holding the gate to be adjusted against the oar during each stroke. Various mechanisms can be used, but the excentric gate and the exchange wedge-gate are the easiest and most precise to handle. Particular attention should be paid to the perpendicular adjustment of the gate-pin.

With the exchange wedge-gate, the areas holding the gate are inserted in the form of small, adjusted wedges (of between – 4° and + 4°) and fixed using small screws. With excentric gates the angle of the area holding the gates is altered by twisting the excentre opposite the body of the gate.

- The larger the angle of the rigger, the more difficult it is to turn the blade of the oar, the less the oar changes angle during a stroke and the smaller the angle of the oar in relation to the water.

- The smaller the angle of the rigger, the further ahead the boat travels with each oar-stroke; the deeper the blade of the oar goes into the water, the more easily the blade of the oar can be turned.

Oars

Most boatbuilders and oar manufacturers supply the long and short oars with a built-in angle of about 3-4° and with standard blade dimensions (Macon or Big Blade). The clubs then merely determine the length and the shape of the blade and in competition rowing, possibly also its flexibility, which can be calculated precisely during manufacture with the aid of new plastics.

The collar is generally adjustable and can be used to adjust the relationship between the oar's inboard and outboard, and hence the amount of leverage exerted on the oar. More recently manufactured oars can also be adjusted a few centimetres in length.

- The longer the oar, the bigger and/or stronger the rower should be, the higher the boat speed should be, the more quickly the oars should be moved at the catch and the turn.

- The shorter the inboard, the longer the blade is in the water during each stroke, the greater the pressure and the higher the speed of each blade at the same rating.

- The longer the inner shank, the easier is the transfer of effort during each stroke, the less the oar is in the water, the more effort is required for the angle of backward lean, and the lower is the speed of each blade at the same rating.

Settings for Boats Based on Experience and Regulations

The following table serves as an overview and aid for adjusting various boats used in training and competition for childrens' and young peoples' rowing, as well as for general and leisure rowing.

The margins for the measurements should be understood as corresponding to the above guidelines. Other settings over and above these are certainly possible, but seldom for racing. Attention must be paid to the fact that the settings for boats for Junior Boys, Junior Girls, Women or Lightweights can be altered; these vary mostly in the length of the oars used.

The following applies to all rowers:

1. Distance between the rower's heels and the lowest part of the sliding seat: 15-20 cm (depending on the the length of the rower's calf).
2. Height of the gate: on a short-oar boat - 15-18 cm (difference between port and starboard side = 0-1.5 cm) on a long-oar boat - 14-17 cm (difference between port and starboard side = 0-1.5 cm).
3. Arrangement of the oars: 0-4° (Big blade: 0-3°).
4. Outward angle of the gate-pin: 0°
5. Total angle: 4-8°.
6. Angle of the base of the stretcher in relation to the boat's longitudinal axis: 40-46°.

Age-group/ Rowing activity	Normal blade (Macon Blade) in cm		Big Blade in cm	
	Short oar	Long oar	Short oar	Long oar
Boys and Girls	285 - 295	370 - 378		
Junior Boys / Junior B Girls	294 - 298	375 - 380		
Junior A Girls	294 - 298	378 - 380	287 - 290	370 - 374
Junior A's	296 - 300	382 - 385	288 - 291	373 - 376
Women's Lightweight	296 - 298	380 - 382	288 - 290	370 - 374
Women	296 - 298	382 - 384	288 - 291	373 - 376
Men's Lightweight	298 - 300	382 - 385	289 - 291	374 - 376
Men	298 - 302	382 - 386	289 - 293	376 - 378
Everyday rowing	295 - 298	375 - 382	288 - 291	374 - 376
Recreational Rowing	295 - 298	375 - 380		

Table 7: Recommended lengths for oars (Macon Blade and Big Blade)

Boats	Thwart distance (TD) in cm	Length of inboard in cm
Racing boats		
1x	158 – 162	87 – 90
2x	158 – 162	87 – 89
4x-/4x+	158 – 160	87 – 88
2-	85 – 87	115 – 117
2+	86 – 87	116 – 118
4-/4+	84 – 86	114 – 116
8+	83 – 84	113 – 115
Tubs		
Sculls	160 – 162	84 – 86
Rowing boats	82 – 84	112 – 114
Junior boats		
Sculls	157 – 160	86 – 87
Rowing boats	85 – 86	115 – 116

Table 8: Boat dimensions and inboard

6. Storing and Care of Boats

When *storing the boats* indoors, care should be taken to put equal stress on all points in contact with the rack. The boat should lie on at least four such points, and the intervals between storage surfaces neither too short nor too long. For this reason it is a good idea to provide for three storage surfaces, i.e. six storage points for the eights. For the four- and two-man boat, the supports are positioned such that each provide support in front of and behind the section of the boat with the outrigger, directly on the fours and 0.5–0.8 m apart on the pairs. In general the boats are stored indoors *keel up*. Single sculls are an exception if they are hung on two pulley slings from the boathouse ceiling.

For storage outdoors various sorts of trestles are used, depending on the purpose of storage:

1. The *normal trestle*: used for storing boats *keel up* in order to clean the body of the boat or for storing the boats until further use.

2. The *belted trestle*: used for holding boats in a relatively stable position *keel down* – in order to clean the boat on the inside or to measure it.

3. The *folding trestle*: like the belted trestle, this is used for storing the boat in the open and for use at regattas.

All trestles should be so constructed that a boat can be stored *keel up* on them.

Starting with newcomers to the sport it is important that rowing equipment (boats and oars) is well cared for. After a rowing session the boat must be sprayed with water and wiped down with a clean wet rag. The oars must also be cleaned with a rag. As a rule no additional substances like detergent or soap are necessary; however, these may be required after rowing through dirty water.

Learning to Row

Regardless of personal motives and areas of application, learning to row requires competent guidance consisting of the mastery of certain rudiments in order to be able to row with other people, and adequate minimum safety standards in the practice of this sport.

Ideas on how *best to learn* to row have a long tradition in this sport. At this point it is not intended to go into the various stages of development and positions. The concept presented here takes these positions into consideration and attempts to do justice to the circumstances existing in clubs and rowing sections of sports clubs. It should be made clear that there are certainly several methods, but reducing a relatively simple task to a *method* should be warned against. The basic principles presented here will have fulfilled their purpose if they are taken as *one* option and helpful encouragement to learn to row. They assume that specialisation only follows after the fundamentals have been mastered (e.g. training in techniques for teenage competition rowers, or specific skills for recreational rowing) and thus is valid for all age groups and abilities.

Of course the differences in learning speed and instruction methods must take into account the learning conditions, previous experience and physical sporting ability. However, it is a declared aim of the fundamentals not to achieve success as soon as possible, but to let *learning to row* in itself become an unforgettable experience and an adventure.

1. Step-by-step Tips on the Basic Principles

The Variety of Boats Available

The coach or sports teacher should make sure that beginners gain experience in all the rudiments of rowing in the various types and categories of boats. Even under optimum conditions instruction in just a one-man boat (scull) is not necessarily the best way of teaching the basics. At the same time it is irrelevant as to whether first experience is gained step-by-step in the team tub, in a boat with long or short oars, or in a skiff. It is not the short learning period for certain movements but rather the varied experience with different boats and oars, as well as differently made-up teams, that are of top priority. The frequently heard remark in teaching people to row *"scull first, then row"* is thus not a binding maxim.

Age-based Instruction (Appropriate to Physical Development)

Rowing can be learned at any age (from eight years) and under almost any conditions; however the best age – as for many other sports – is between ten and thirteen years of age. Clubs must take this into consideration when offering rowing. The choice and emphasis of training and even equipment should be appropriate to the stages of development of the young people involved (e.g. the dimensions of the boat and the oars).

Demonstrating the Movements

A correct idea of the movements, combined with the knowledge of their purpose, is of enormous help to the beginning rower. Direct feedback (e.g. in balancing the skiff) is often hailed as the best teacher, but should be complemented by instructional films or videos on the sequence of movements.

The most effective and the recognised first step for beginners is probably the demonstration by the coach him- or herself. When demonstrating the sequence of movements, care should be taken to emphasise those that are essential. The carrying out of these movements should not be ossified in a single form, thereby becoming an end in themselves. It is not the barely comprehensible aesthetic movement (i.e. form) that counts, but rather the intended function. Movements and exercises accompanied by explanations should at the same time also be combined with the necessary technical language. Here care should be taken that this be done clearly and in doses appropriate to the age of the participants.

Complete Movement Sequences

Rowing movements should always be taught as a cyclical movement sequence and not in separate, part movements, either in the boat or in the rowing tank. The explanations of the sequence of movements should always contain a few words about their function or intention, which may be connected with an invitation to those present to find solutions on an individual basis.

Movement Task

Exercises and goals should be set to complement every learning step or element of movement sequences. A range of games and competitions present themselves here which not only serve to consolidate the sequences learned, but also to motivate the rowers-to-be, and to liven up the instruction.

Organisation

Depending on the circumstances and the conditions in the area where rowing is practised, the number of beginners varies for coaches. On a heavily-frequented stretch of water with a strong current the coach cannot supervise more than four beginners (he coxes the four); on a lake protected from the wind which is also relatively calm (for getting back into the boat) up to twelve beginners can be looked after. The right location for instruction should be chosen by the coach in order to look after the material the boat is made of, as well as to ensure safety. Basically he/she can select a place on land (on the landing-stage) or on the water (in the boat as cox or as one of the rowers, as an escort in a skiff or in a motorboat). The sketches on the next two pages indicate a few basic options (fig. 5).

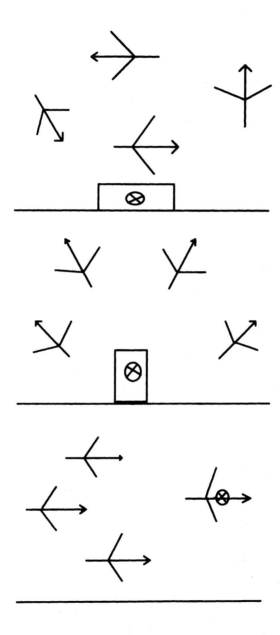

Figure 5

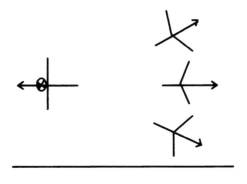

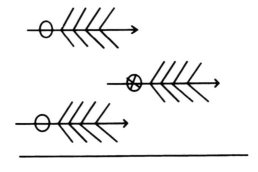

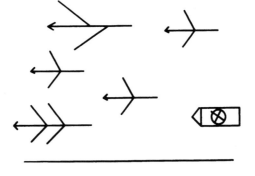

Figure 6

2. The Basics of Learning to Row

Irrespective of personal motives or objectives, there are still seven steps in the fundamentals of learning to row for the beginner (and hence for the coach giving the instruction as well), which build on one another, and the mastery of which is necessary for all areas of rowing, whether the beginner decides in favour of competitive or leisure rowing.

Basics of Learning to Row
1) Familiarisation with rowing equipment and how to handle it
2) Ensuring proper balance
3) Rowing in a forwards direction
4) Manoeuvering the boat
5) Overcoming difficult situations
6) Steering
7) Introduction to the various areas of rowing.

The Basics 1: Familiarisation with and Handling of Rowing Equipment

Before boating with beginners, a tour of the club's boathouse is recommended. With the help of the boats stored there, the various *types of boats, oars and categories of boats* can be explained. As well, a boat can be put on the trestles in order to illustrate the function and use of individual parts such as the *slide, stretcher, rigger, gate* and of course the *oars*. At the same time an explanation of how the materials used in boat-making have developed over boating's 160-year history should not be forgotten.

Further instructions concern carrying the boats to the landing-stage and the water respectively. It is essential that when carrying the boat two rowers of approximately the same height stand opposite each other on each side at the bow and stern, not inside the area of the rigger. At this stage the skiff is carried by two people, each standing about 1–1.5 m from each end of the boat. This prevents the boat from swinging to and fro. After the oars have been brought to the landing-stage they must be laid down so that they are not in danger of damage.

Different ways of carrying sculls for beginners (above) and advanced rowers (below)

The boat is first carried by hand out of the boat house and then to the landing-stage on the shoulders. As a rule tubs are put into the water keel down over the landing-stage or over a roll fixed to the landing-stage; narrow boats such as plastic skiffs are laid sideways into the water.

The coach demonstrates how oars are put in the gates: they are set at the narrowest part of the shaft – the neck of the blade – and then pushed up to the *button*. The oars, which point to the water, are laid across the top of the hull into the boat. Care should be taken not to confuse *port side* and *starboard* oars and to have the gates pointing sternwards.

This first stage is concluded with an explanation of how to climb into the boat and the correct position of the stretcher. When climbing into the boat the rower must remember to step only on the correct place, i.e. the footboard between both slide-paths while holding on to the oars with the hand nearest the water. The sliding seat remains behind the heel of the foot on the footboard, and the other hand remains firmly on the inside of the rigger or on the landing-stage itself.

It is always a good idea for beginners to get in one after the other while the coach holds the boat from the landing-stage.

The stretchers are adjusted when the boat sets out from the landing-stage (i.e. when it is on the water). Here the oar-handles are jammed between the upper body and the thighs while the rower's legs are laid over the top of the side of the boat, or in a tub on the footboards.

The stretcher can be adjusted manually by loosening its screws. The rule of thumb for the adjusting of the stretcher in boats for which short oars are used is: sitting with stretched legs and leaning back slightly. The rower should just be able to pull the handles of the oars past his body. In a boat using longer oars the inboard of the oar should not pass the upper body.

The Basics 2: Ensuring Proper Balance

The boat is now sitting on the water and the rowers have assumed the basic or safety position. With the oar-blades lying flat on the water, the beginners sit in the boat with their legs stretched out and holding the oars over their knees.

This basic or *safety position* is assumed every time a sequence of movements has been completed. With the help of the oar-blades turned over to lie flat on the water, all types of balancing exercises can now be performed. While these make clear the wobbly nature of the boat to the beginner, they should also gradually give a feeling of safety. Favourite forms of exercises are, for example, when the coach tries – in vain – to overturn the boat.

The rowers hold the boat fast by holding the oars up in the air or pressing both inboards into the boat and letting it tip from one side to the other. One essential experience, including for later exercises, is influencing the position of the boat by balancing it with the oars. If the rowers raise one side of the boat in the port side direction while the blades are lying flat on the water, the boat tips in a starboard direction. The reverse is also the case.

Getting into a skiff

The Basics 3: Rowing in a Forwards Direction

The free-floating oar-blade can now be positioned vertically and drawn on one side gently towards the rower's body. In this way one can *feel the correct position of the blade* in the water and the correct path of the oar in the water respectively. At the same time the hand doing the rowing is always above the hand resting on the thigh. During this one-sided forward-rowing in which the seat cannot – or can hardly – be rolled, the coach should already be keeping an eye on the correct positions of the rowers' hands on the oars. When turning the oar in a vertical direction, only the fingers should be wrapped around the handle. The inner surfaces of the hand do not touch the handle and the wrist remains straight (i.e. the surfaces of the hands and the lower arms form a straight line). When done with the right and left hands alternately, these exercises can soon be carried out with the whole team in a skiff in many different positions.

Indispensible for forwards rowing in skiffs – which, though possible in tubs at this point, but not yet necessary – is the raising and lowering of the oar-blades. Dragging of the blades on the water causes skiffs (and tubs) to assume a relatively stable position. While errors in the control of oar-blades when rowing a skiff are immediately noticeable, this is not necessarily the case when rowing a tub. For this reason great emphasis should be laid on the correct position of the hands, to which those with little practice do not necessarily adapt immediately when turning the oar-blades. The lower arms become easily cramped and the wrists get strained, so that constant hints from the coach, small breaks and rowing the tub with squared oar-blades, can be helpful.

At this stage of the basics the seat travels further along the slide-path with every oar-stroke. Both oars are at this stage drawn towards the body, raised out of the water and, with the blades trailing along the top of the water, are brought down for the next catch. The inboards, which usually overlap each other, are drawn one behind the other and over one another (i.e. the left hand is – from the point of view of the rower – somewhat behind and over the right hand). Both in the tub and in the skiff a series of exercises designed to stabilise the sequences of movements can now be considered, which all the rowers should also learn. Thus, the direction of the boat can be influenced by pulling a bit more on one side than the other. The rowers can row in pairs, in threes and perhaps even as a whole team, and in combination with the exercises in stage 2, row towards a destination. This part of the basics includes the ability to brake the moving boat relatively quickly, i.e. stopping it on one or both sides.

The Basics 4: Manoeuvering the Boat

The next step now consists of being able to carry out the most important manoeuvres in the boat. On the basis of previous experience, "backing it down" lends itself as a suitable starting exercise. As with rowing forwards, the slide distance is constantly increased as the rower becomes more confident. The oars are pushed away from the body into the starting position, with the curve of the oar-blade positioned towards the stern.

Together with forward-rowing, backing-it-down is the prerequisite for turning, which, depending on the rowers' learning ability, can now be introduced in several different variations and partial steps. Of course time should also be made at this stage for little games and competitions.

The next step is learning to land and set off on one's own from the landing-stage. At the beginning the coach pushes or pulls the beginners' sculls near the landing-stage, or coxes the boat. Now it is up to the beginners to discover and practise appropriate ways of landing and boating in different conditions.

The safety position in a skiff

The Basics 5: Overcoming Difficult Situations

At this stage the rowers anticipate and practise difficult situations, which can occur in various areas of rowing or which are required in order to perform certain techniques. In a scull it is necessary to acquire a degree of safety, e.g. by *"flying"*, by holding the boat while letting go of the inner loom, standing up or even trying to do a headstand. Getting back into the scull after an involuntary wetting should also be practised, if this has not been done so far. This contributes to the safety of the rower as well as careful use of the equipment.

Other aspects of overcoming difficult situations are: navigating a way through narrows and under bridges where the oars must be drawn in and held against the side of the boat; how to row and what to do when caught in waves made by other boats (rowing boats are generally positioned parallel to the waves and the rowers assume the safety position); and changing places in the boat as well as landing at different types of banks.

Bringing the oars alongside the boat

The Basics 6: Steering

Every newcomer to rowing should make use of the opportunity to lead a rowing team as cox. Apart from steering the boat itself (i.e. keeping it on the right course or changing direction), the cox has to ensure the safety of the team by using the right commands.

Every beginner to elementary rowing training should try steering a boat towards a given destination under all kinds of different conditions (wind, waves, current, the load in the boat, the position of the rudder, etc). In this way he very quickly realises the necessity and function of the commands used in steering.

Although there is a tendency in competitive rowing to continually reduce the number of boats with a cox, the coxed boat (two-, four- and eight-man) is the rule in day-to-day club operations. However, the following rules apply for the so-called coxless boat; both for those steered by the use of a scull on both sides (single and double sculls), as well for those fitted with a foot-controlled rudder and steered by a single rower (e.g. doubles, fours and quads).

The following *steering rules* should be observed:

1. A change of direction with the rudder is only possible when the boat is travelling faster than the water it is being rowed on.

2. Steering first of all means a loss of speed. For this reason the rudder should be used as little as possible and with one's eye on a distant rather than a close orientation point.

3. The rudder-line should only be pulled on when the blades are out of the water. Blades *in the water* make it not only a lot more difficult to steer, the steering also has a strong braking effect on the boat.

4. The rudder should be applied lightly and at a gentle angle so that the balance of the boat is not upset.

5. The rudder-line must not be wound around the cox's body. It is held with the hands on the top of the hull – especially in racing boats – and should be kept under constant tension. This applies especially to backing it down.

6. In long and high waves the boat must be positioned parallel to the waves and the rowers should assume the safety position until the boat has passed through the waves.

7. The boat should always come into the landing-stage against the current. The only exceptions are in a very weak current and when a very strong wind is blowing against the direction of the current.

Turning in a Strong Current

The boat can be turned just as easily with the current as against it. When rowing *with the current* the rower can stop the boat on the side nearer the bank, thereby bringing the boat's stern into the current, which assists the turning process. Turning *against the current* is best done by stopping the boat on one side and pointing the bows into the stream. It must be remembered, however, that the current will carry the boat further.

Putting in at a landing-stage

Putting in With and Without Use of Wind

The landing-stage can be approached in calm waters at a relatively acute angle. The oars on the side of the boat facing the river act as a brake, thereby bringing the boat around. The blades on the side facing the bank are raised, and the rowers stop the boat by grabbing the landing-stage with their hands. The cox gets out first, holds the boat firmly and then gives the crew the command to get out.

If a boat can land on either side of a landing-stage it must be borne in mind that in strong winds, when putting in on the side facing the prevailing wind (the windward side), the boat can be quickly pressed against the landing-stage. The boat should therefore approach the landing-stage at the appropriate angle.

It is more difficult to put in on the leeward side. The boat is pressed away from the landing-stage, which may require several attempts, but which can also be easier on the material of the boat. In strong winds, the boat should be tied up on the leeward side with a line at the rudder and the bow so the wind cannot blow it against the landing-stage.

The Basics 7: An Introduction to the Various Areas of Rowing

The conclusion of training in the fundamentals comprises an overview of the various areas of rowing. On the one hand the knowledge gained can be applied on unfamiliar waters with the help of one-day or weekend excursions. Alternatively, it opens the door to the various other areas of rowing, e.g. recreational rowing.

One can move fairly easily into individual areas of rowing, but every rower should be allowed to become acquainted with these areas and come back to them from time to time at certain intervals. Recreational rowers should also be told about rowing as a fitness sport and even take up the club's offers in this area. For the would-be competitive rower even day-trips or longer recreational trips on unfamiliar waters can become an unforgettable experience.

Finally the leisure rower will also want to fall back on those games, competitions and events available during the transition from being a beginner to becoming a competitive rower.

PARTIAL GOALS	SPECIALIST TERMS	TIPS/CORRECTION
Information: the main types of boats and oars, appropriate rowing clothing	Tubs, sculls, oars, gate, rigger, sliding seat, slide, stretcher	Rowing clothing
Oars rudder	Blade, shaft, rudder, sleeve (of oar), rudder-line	Storing the boat
Handling the equipment, carrying the boat	Bow, stern, hull saxboard	Looking after the boat, carrying position
Putting the boat into the water, lifting the boat out of the water	Keel, fin	Tubs should be in an up-turned position; pay attention to the (position of the) rigger; pay attention to the fin of plastic boats.
Putting the oars in the gates	Port, Starboard side	Is each oar on the correct side? Are the gates in the right place? The oar blade should lie on the landing-stage with the curve upwards.
Getting in and out of the boat	Stretcher, footboards	Is the oar fixed tight? Are the gates done up? Note the position of the sliding-seat. Do not stand in the bottom of the boat.
Personal adjustments	Inboard, stretcher, stretcher screw	Are the screws tight? Correct position at backstop

Table 9: An overview of The Basics 1: Familiarisation with and Handling of Rowing Equipment

Rowing Commands

1. "Hands on! – Are you ready? – Lift!"
2. "Turning! – Are you ready? – Turn!"
3. "Crew! – Port side! – Starboard!: – Getting in! – Pushing off!"
4. "Crew! – Port side! – Starboard!: – Getting out ... now!"
5. "Numbering off from bow!"

Exercises

Exercises in Observation

How do the other rowers do it (e.g. getting into the boat, carrying it, etc.)?

What's an easy way to remember which oars go on which side?

	SPECIALIST TERMS	TIPS/CORRECTIONS
Basic position, safety position	Handles, inboard	Are the blades lying flat on the water? Position of the inboards at the same height?
Balancing and rocking exercises		Are the gates closed? Is the boat out of the way of other craft?
Feeling the position of the blades		Are fingers and hands in the right position on the oar?
Rowing forwards on one side and backwards on the other side alternately	Squared blades, catch	Blade position, position of hands and fingers, hand movement? The hand doing the rowing is carried over the hand at rest.

Table 10: An overview of The Basics 2: Ensuring Proper Balance

Exercises and Games

1. Lay the blades on the water, hold the oar handles tightly above your thighs and try to make the boat rock by swinging your body to and fro.
2. Do this again and try letting go of the oars for a moment.
3. Turn the oars into a horizontal position, press both their inboards into the boat and rock your upper body from one side to the other (= feathering the blades).
4. Hold the blades lying on the water and rock the boat by alternately moving your hands up and down.

PARTIAL GOALS	SPECIALIST TERMS	TIPS/CORRECTIONS
Squaring and feathering	Square, feather and finish	How to hold the oars
Steadily increasing use of the slide	Front stops, backstops, stroke	Is the body posture cramped? Position of the hands, hand movement, control of the oars, use of the slide, length of the slide
Minor direction changes by pulling harder on one side	A little harder on port side, ditto on starboard	Exaggerated movements, catch, length of stroke
Braking, stopping	Holding it hard	Position of oar-blades? Stopping gradually
Rowing towards a set point	Keeping on course	

Table 11: An overview of The Basics 3: Rowing in a Forwards Direction

Rowing Commands

1. "Front stops: – Are you ready? – Go!"
2. "A little harder on port/starboard side !"
3. "Easy all!"
4. "Blades on the water!"
5. "Ready to hold ... hold it hard!"

Exercises and Games

1. Close your eyes and square and feather the blades several times. Are the grip and the position of the blade still correct?
2. Rowing with squared blade:
   - by yourself
   - in pairs
   - all together
   - in pairs with one oar squared and the other feathered
   - in pairs with one oar sliding along the top of the water, the other *completely out of the water.*
3. Row five (or three) strokes harder on the port side. Change sides. Bow pair/three and four, etc. Pull harder on the port or starboard side.
4. When is the best time to look around and check that you are on course?
5. How do you find your way on the water?
6. Who has to look around the least when making your way to a fixed point?
7. Who can row left/right in a circle? Take five (3,2,1) strokes in the water with your right and left hands alternately!

PARTIAL GOALS	SPECIALIST TERMS	TIPS/CORRECTIONS
Backing it down on both sides while gradually using more of the slide		Position of the blades, hands; hand movement
Port side and starboard turns	Turn	Same speed for those rowing forwards and those backing it down
Pushing off from and landing at the landing-stage	Wind, waves, current	Angle of approach, stopping too soon, too late? Lack of attention to conditions?

Table 12: An overview of The Basics 4: Manoeuvering the Boat

Rowing Commands

1. *"Whole crew backing it down! Are you ready? - Go!"*
2. *"Portside/starboard side ... turn!"*
3. *"Portside/starboard side: blades up!"*

Exercises and Games

1. As for rowing forwards: the crew backs it down towards an objective.
2. Three strokes forward on the port side and three strokes backwards on the starboard side.
3. One stroke forwards on the port side and one stroke backwards on the starboard side alternately.
4. Complete turns to port and starboard sides.
5. Who can do a turn (180° or 360°) with the fewest oar strokes?
6. Who turned 360° three times the fastest (both sides)?
7. Combination exercise: the crew backs it down about 50 m towards an objective, performs a 360° turn and rows on forwards.

Approaching a landing stage in a scull

Preparing to get out of a scull

Getting out of a scull

8. If possible, put in at a landing-stage from various directions backwards and forwards.
9. Try putting in under various conditions (e.g. in wind, heavier waters and waves, and when there are other boats on the water).
10. How do competition rowers and other rowers in the club do this?
11. Reducing speed using the oars on one or both sides.
12. Who can stop the closest to a line or to the landing-stage?
13. How do the experts (competition rowers) row towards the landing-stage?

PARTIAL GOALS	SPECIALIST TERMS	TIPS/CORRECTIONS
Advanced balancing exercises in a scull	Blades feathered in the air coming forward	Are the rowers taking the oars out of the water the right way? Is the speed sufficient?
Rowing in waves	Feathering high Blades up and away	Has the crew assumed the safety position? Distance between the boat and other craft on the water? Distance between the boat and the river-bank? Is the boat parallel to the waves?
Changing places in the boat	Transverse rib, stretcher	Safety position of those seated in the boat. Those changing place should not step on the bottom of the boat.
Rowing through narrow spots	All oars in	Is there enough run on the boat? Is the crew holding on to the handles?
Getting back into the boat after falling into the water		Are the oars parallel to the boat and properly fixed to the boat? Is the seat at the bow-end of the slide?

Table 13: An overview of The Basics 5: Overcoming Difficult Situations

Rowing Commands

> 1. *"Feather high!"*
> 2. *"Oars longways!"*

Exercises and Games

1. Who can row three strokes forward then let the boat run with the blades feathered?
2. Who can "fly" fast over the longest distance?
3. Who can stand up in the boat?
4. Who can let go of the inboards of the oar while doing this?
5. Who can let go of the inboards and position the sculls *parallel* to the boat?
6. Who can row through a narrow stretch of water (or between two posts) without scraping the oars?
7. Who can row as closely as possible to a buoy (or the landing-stage or a pile) with the oars positioned parallel to the boat?
8. Who can lie down in the boat?

9. Slalom course: row forwards through buoys, doing 180° turns, rowing backwards towards an objective, reducing speed, rowing under an obstacle, picking an object up out of the water, throwing a ball into a bucket, etc.
10. Drifting ball: push a big beachball around on the water using hands and oars.
11. Perform orienteering exercises on small excursions.

PARTIAL GOALS	SPECIALIST TERMS	TIPS/CORRECTIONS
Knowledge of rowing commands	Rowing commands	Does everybody understand them? Are the commands appropriate to the situation?
Knowledge and use of the steering rules		Is the rudder pulled at too sharp an angle? Sudden pulls on the rudder-line. Does the cox steer towards a far-off objective?
Putting in at and setting out from the landing-stage as cox, using the rowing commands		

Table 14: An overview of The Basics 6: Steering

Exercises and Games

1. Carrying out all steering manoeuvres with the help of the rowing commands but without using the rudder.
2. Steering towards a specific objective (e.g. landing) without the rudder.
3. Leading a crew from the boathouse onto the water, carrying out a training session and then leading the crew back to the boathouse.

An Overview of The Basics 7: An Introduction to the Various Areas of Rowing

Hints and advice on individual areas of rowing, like rowing excursions, rowing as a sport promoting fitness and health, and various forms of stress and competitive rowing are set out in Part 3 of the book. As a conclusion to the fundamentals of rowing, coaches or other rowers in the club can show the now-advanced rowers the following:

1. Excursions (Day and Weekend Excursions)

At the conclusion of the fundamentals a day trip of about 25–30 km in length can be held. A date for a weekend trip can be set the same evening after returning.

2. Rowing as a Sport Promoting Fitness and as a Balance to Other Aspects of Life

The coach gives information about existing groups in the club that pursue these goals. An introduction to the theory of rowing and health, nutrition, etc and integration into general club activities can be made.

3. Competitive Rowing in a Rowing Club

A systematic introduction not only to the opportunities but also the dangers of fitness training for rowing should be offered. Supplementary forms of exercise and training resources are presented under expert guidance. These supplemental forms may be found in a training room or through indoor or artificial rowing (i.e. on rowing machines, in rowing tanks, on a jogging track, etc). Practice and training times are announced. For those interested, information is given on possible forms of competition and events making the appropriate physical demands on the participants (e.g. rowing for everyone, long-distance rowing, cross-country, club rowing excursions, rowing triathlons, etc).

3. Rowing Safely

The main cause of rowing accidents are collisions with other boats, or with obstacles in or on the water. Although there are safety regulations for rowing in most clubs and on the most dangerous regatta courses for each rowing and training area, accidents occur again and again.

To avoid these accidents it is advisable for those in the bow of a boat to look around fairly frequently, even when the boat has a cox. Especially the young and often small coxes cannot see certain areas in front of the bow through the rowers sitting in front of them.

A further more frequent area where accidents occur is the failure to predict the weather. In this way even tub boats can fill with water in seconds in an approaching storm on lakes or wide areas of water subject to windgusts. The observations and advice of local rowers should therefore be taken seriously.

In an approaching storm, the boat should immediately make for the riverbank or lakeside and excursions or training sessions should be called off. Rowers should also stay close to the riverbank in cold weather and low water temperatures at all costs. In winter, competitive rowers – particularly when using small, easily capsizible boats – should only go onto the water when accompanied by the coach in a motorboat.

The danger of not being able to swim to the riverbank in case of the boat being filled with water by waves or tipping over should not be underestimated, given the risk of exposure. In such cases it is generally recommended that, since the boat never completey sinks, one rower should remain with it and try to attract attention by making himself seen and heard. If long trips in risky waters or lakes are planned, one should always inform club members about the destination of the trip and the estimated time of return.

It goes without saying that an entry concerning the trip in a club's trip-log before setting out is compulsory. If worse comes to worst a rescue operation can be started more quickly with the help of the information recorded there.

These are only a few of the basic safety problems related to rowing. Special situations such as what to do in locks, for example, require specific instruction, which must be taken care of by the coach before embarking on such trips. The problem of appropriate rowing attire is addressed in another chapter on the various areas of rowing.

PART 2: ROWING TECHNIQUE AND TRAINING

Technique

1. The Problem of the "Right" Rowing Technique

When watching very good rowers and and rowing teams, it is easy to see that not everyone agrees on the *best* rowing technique. A whole range of variations can be identified, but an analysis of these would only serve to make generalisations on technique. *Good* rowing techniques, apart from sporting purposes, fulfill two main tasks:

1. To use the rower's constitution and fitness in order to enhance the speed of the boat (the effective forward driving force).

2. To minimise the force and movements that counter the effective driving force or that lead to higher energy use during rowing (resistance reduction).

In order to generate a forward driving force under the prevailing conditions and to reduce resistance, the problem consists of finding a compromise between the constitution and physical fitness of the rower and the objectives of rowing. The rower's technique is a compromise made either by the coach or the rower him- or herself, in order to fulfill a certain task. In contrast to those sports in which the performance of movement is also judged (e.g. gymnastics and figure skating), performance in rowing is based on other criteria. It is also difficult to talk about *right* or *wrong*, or *good* or *bad* technique without knowing what the terms of reference are.

It should also be quite clear that the definition of *good* rowing technique changes from time to time: the best rowers in the world row differently today compared to their predecessors of 15 to 20 years ago and quite differently compared to their predecessors of 50 to 60 years ago. In each era people thought they knew the correct rowing technique. Even today fierce arguments break out between coaches and rowers over what "*good*" technique should be, and there are arguments and counter-arguments for all points-of-view.

Rowing technique must always be viewed in the context of

a) the scarcely alterable physical requirements (constitution) of the rower (e.g. physical size, length of the limbs, body-weight).

b) the variable requirements relating to the rower's constitution (e.g. strength, endurance, flexibility).

c) the objectives (e.g. recreational rowing, rowing in very heterogeneous groups, races of 2000 m or even 5000 m in length).

d) the available boat and oar materials.

e) the views, attitudes and knowledge of coaches and national and regional rowing associations.

f) the techniques of the currently leading rowing nations.

2. Principles of Rowing Technique

There is a whole series of requirements originating from the field of physics if a rower a) wishes to produce the most effective forward driving force, and b) keep the resulting resistance as low as possible. Biomechanical investigations into the problem of rowing technique have found that the movement of the oar-blade produces not only a forward drivingforce when it moves against the direction the boat is travelling but also when it moves laterally to the direction the boat is travelling (similar to a ship's propellor). When top rowers make an oar stroke, the blade of the oar moves approximately 1.6 m – 1.9 m laterally to the direction of the boat, but only 50-60 cm against the direction the boat is travelling. From this lateral movement, which can only be reached by very large angles of forward reach and backward lean, the rower can expect more impetus.

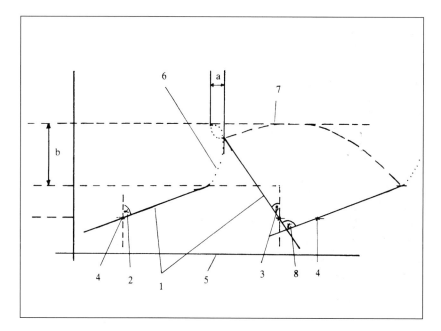

1. Oar
2. Angle of forward lean
3. Angle of backward lean
4. Gate-pin
5. Centre of boat

6. Path of the tip of the oar blade in the water
7. Path of the tip of the oar blade out of the water
8. Angle of effort
   a. "Slip" (longways movement of the oar blade)
   b. Crossways movement of the oar blade

Figure 7

The resistance on a travelling boat is enormous. In order to minimise this, a certain average and constant speed of the boat, requiring negligible energy use, should be aimed at. As the impetus in rowing is intermittent and incontinuous, requiring relatively powerful movements in the boat on the part of the rower and the oars, physical demand cannot be met. Speed fluctuations accompanied by increased resistance and enormous energy loss are unavoidable in rowing.

Maximum and minimum boat speed varies by up to 25% from the average speed. The boat reaches top speed during the forwards rolling phase, and the lowest speed shortly after the insertion of the oars into the water.

Good rowing technique is distinguished by keeping speed fluctuations as low as possible. The fewer the fluctuations, the higher the average speed is at the same energy use. This is made possible by a constant speed of the parts being moved, negligible acceleration, and generally little movement of mass in the boat.

In spite of all limitations on *optimal* rowing technique, a series of *technical principles* can be distinguished on the basis of this knowledge, which almost all top rowers and rowing teams display. In a manner of speaking they form the lowest common denominator in the description of rowing technique, and serve as a starting point for many (still possible) variations.

First Principle

Outstanding rowers and crews distinguish themselves by a very long oar stroke. Their angle of effort (area of travel covered by the oar) in a scull is approximately between 100–110° and 90–100° in a rowboat.

Second Principle

In world-class rowing the first part of the movement of the oar is of central importance: thus, the angle in front of the gate is about twice as large as the area behind it. The catching and the lock-on occur very quickly.

Third Principle

All top rowers try to produce as little vertical movement as possible when rowing.

Fourth Principle

In first class boats, effort is made to move the body, hands, oars and sliding-seat with uniform speed and acceleration while avoiding reaching-out speeds.

Fifth Principle

Internationally successful teams distinguish themselves by having good team coordination: work on the water, physical exercise and work on the slide present a unified image.

Using these principles, the very close connection between health and physical fitness and the techniques of top-class rowing becomes clear. For successful top-class rowing, very tall athletes with relatively long arms and/or trunks have great advantages.

These requirements are supplemented and compensated for by great flexibility, especially in the shoulders, as well as an excellent feeling for body and movement. For continual and economic effort over the whole distance of the race, cardio-pulmonary endurance is a deciding factor, as well as above-average strength.

3. The Sequence of Movements during Rowing

The following descriptions of movements and sketches of movement sequences, have been developed to a large extent by NOLTE (1985), and serve as an *ideal portrayal* of the sequence of movements in competitive rowing.

The Sequence of Movements when Sculling (Figs. 7-11)

The backward lean

The maximum backward lean is reached when the rower can exert just enough effort on the oar and can start to lift the oars smoothly out of the water. In this position the hands must be pulled towards the shoulders. In this position the legs are almost fully stretched and the upper body is bent slightly backwards.

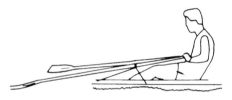

Figure 7

Rolling the body forward

Current principles of technique say that the forward movement of the body should be carried out in such a manner that no great acceleration or speed fluctuations at the sculls or through the rower occur. The hands come in and go out at about the same speed and then accompany the upper body forwards in a vertical direction.

As soon as the hands are in front of the knees, the rower brings the oars into the water with an even and simultaneous movement of the knee and hip joints.

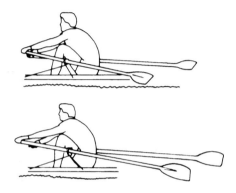

Figure 8

Once the rower's hands have squared the blades in parallel, roughly on the last third of the slide, maximum reach can be achieved by stretching the shoulder joints.

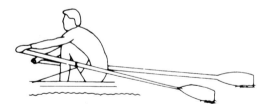

Figure 9

The catch　Putting the oars into the water takes place through the upwards movement of the hands. Dipping the oars into the water must take place in the shortest time possible with the pulling force on the oar-handle adjusted to the situation. This force attains its maximum (about 10-20°) in front of the right-angled position. The oars should be vertical to the boat's longitudinal axis.

After the rowing movement is completed, the knees and hips begin to stretch, while the arms are bent in a right-angled position.

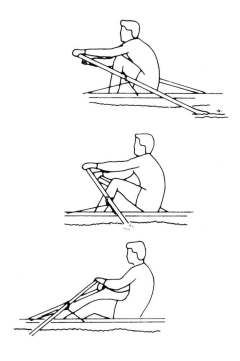

Figure 10

The finish

The final draw on the oars, and the withdrawing of the oars from the water, takes place first of all through use of the arms and shoulders. The hands are drawn down in a slightly rearwards motion, supported by the shoulders and a slight lean back. At the same time the oar-blades are raised out of the water and feathered.

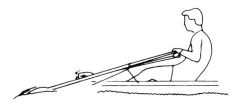

Figure 11

Notes on Rowing with Oars

Rowing with oars differs from sculling only in a few points, but the same principles apply.

Holding the oar: The outer hand grips the end of the oar-handle and there is a gap of about 1.5 – 2 hand-breadths between both hands. Squaring and feathering are carried out by the hand on the inside.

The shoulder: The angle of the shoulder follows the inboard and turns when bringing the oar perpendicular to the boat. To support this position the outer leg is slightly splayed.

The upper body: For optimal use of drawing power the upper part of the body must follow the circuit of the inboard in a circular path. In order to keep vertical movement as negligible as possible, the whole oar-movement is carried out with slightly rounded back.

When leaning back at the finish, the rower should take care that his/her upper body does not bend sideways parallel to the inboard. The angle of the shoulder remains vertical to the boat.

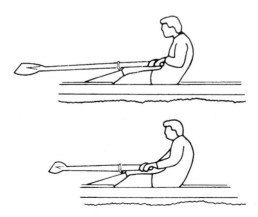

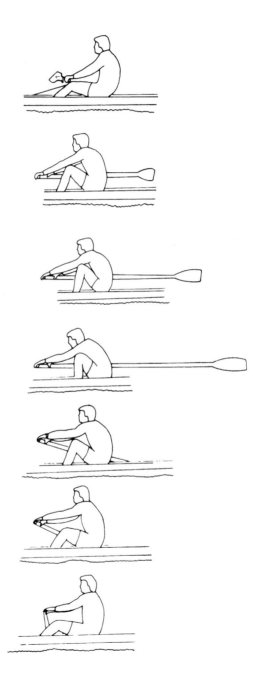

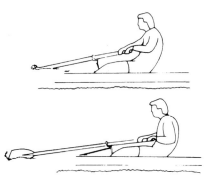

Figure 12

The following ideal schematic illustrations serve to clarify the main features of rowing technique:

1. Angle of the body when at maximum compression and at a fully drawn finish

β= 20–30°

α = 45–60°
     55–60°
γ = 0–10°
     0–5°

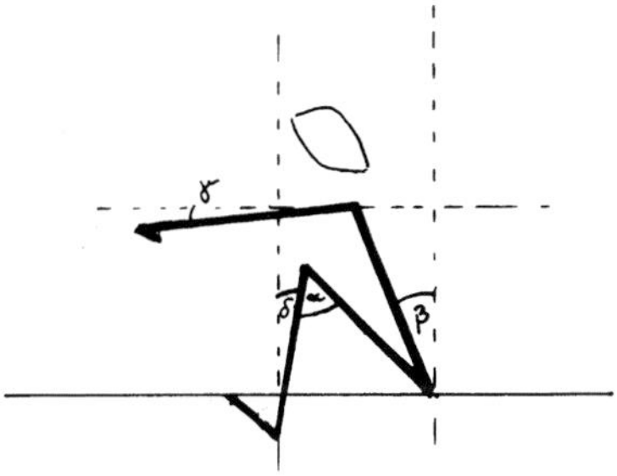

Figure 13

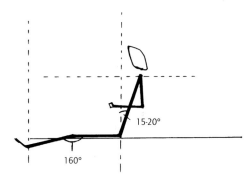

Figure 14

The position of the body at the catch

2. An idealised curve of hand movement during a rowing stroke

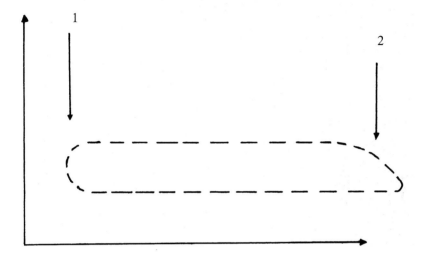

Figure 15

4. The Main Principles of Developing Rowing Technique

Teaching rowing technique is made considerably easier if a few methodical tips are observed. These tips are guided by two main principles:

1. The coach must have a clear idea of the principles of the sequence of movements during each stroke.

2. Developing proficient movement (rowing technique) must be task-related and not an end in itself.

Hints on Methods and Organisational Matters

- When talking to those taking part in practice, the coach should take into consideration their ages, levels of knowledge and motivation.

- Apart from descriptions and explanations of movements, kinesthetic perception (feeling movement, awareness of one's body) should also be taken into consideration. In other words rowing should also be presented as an experience. Such experiences contribute to the more precise idea of movement and to the improvement of the memory of movement.

- The coach should also graphically (e.g. visually or aurally) illustrate movement sequences by demonstrating them to those present at practice.

- Getting through the tasks should always be carried out in the light of each individual's ability (age, height, weight, etc). The coach should not demand the impossible.

- Coaching as well as correcting errors should initially concentrate on the essentials. The coach should not get bogged down in petty matters or in details.

- In every phase of instruction in technique, attention should be paid to the large list of movement exercises. A premature, stereotyped use of the cyclical movement sequence (e.g. only rowing forwards) can easily prevent further development of movement.

- Besides coaching in technique, physical fitness must also be developed. Both factors are mutually dependent, i.e. if one is neglected, the development of the other is restricted. Similar to movement exercises, the development of physical fitness should always be determined by the trainees' development, their individual goals and personal qualities.

5. Rowing Errors and how to Correct Them

Before the coach corrects the rowers' mistakes, he should be aware to what extent he himself is the cause of the problem. This may happen if he incorrectly explains or demonstrates a movement because of an insufficient understanding of a movement or a lack of ability. In addition, physical training conditions should also be borne in mind. For example, wind and waves can cause fear in beginners, which then makes the absorption of information more difficult. The following list of errors (see p. 90) has the principles of technique as its point of reference. Besides the possible causes and effects, corrective measures are given, which can, of course, be extended. For all the errors given here, hints on correction follow and, for this reason, are not listed here.

The Main Corrective Measures

- Compare one's own understanding of movement with those of the trainee and let him/her comment on his/her own movements and those of others using videos or personal observation.

- Have the trainees carry out the movements and movement sequences at varying speeds and in varying sequences, e.g. in slow motion, with breaks, as isolated parts of a whole movement or at full speed.

- Create conditions or give exercises that make errors impossible, e.g. get the rowers to row with the oar blade turned up if they turn it down in the water.

- Exaggerate the corrections to mistakes, e.g. get the trainees to row with an extremely upright trunk if they exert their hips and legs before putting pressure on the oar-blade!

- Encourage general physical development (strengthening) as well as technical training, e.g. by taking part in other sports, but also by means of special strengthening exercises.

- Make use of competition with the help of a stopwatch – especially with children and teenagers. Through excessive dwelling at the *artificial* beginners' level (slow and easy practice with constant comments from the coach) the rowers are accustomed to these movement sequences so that they find it difficult to learn movements which are quicker, more powerful and appropriate to the situation later on.

- Vary boat types, oar-types, situations and partners.

PROBLEM	EFFECTS	POSSIBLE CAUSES
Angle of rower's legs too small when leaning forward	Insufficient work in the water, insufficient forward driving force ("push"), uneconomic use of effort	Stretcher incorrectly adjusted (height, angle, longitudinal direction); lack of flexibility on the part of the rower, gate not high enough, insufficient body height, inboards too small, feeling of insecurity when legs are stretched out
Angle of rower's forward lean too great	Encourages "bum-shoving"* rower ducks trunk of body when stretched out	Stretcher or heel-rest set too low, trunk of body between knees
Backward lean too small	Insufficient room for oar- stroke, no room for inboard and hands	Distance between slide and gate, dimensions of the inboards, strength in upper body and shoulders
Upper body leans over inboard	Oar stroke not balanced, reduction of forward thrust, messy finish	Muscles in shoulder and upper body under-developed, position of the head

*For explanation see p. 92.

Table 15: First principle: a long oar stroke

Possible Remedies

1. Check the dimensions of the boat, adjust the oars and the distance between the gates.
2. Flexibility training.
3. Balancing exercises (in case of any lack of confidence).
4. Strengthening of the shoulder and back muscles.
5. Rowing with fixed seat and squared blades with a gradual lengthening of the oar-stroke.
6. Let the trainees row with a crew that can row correctly.

Rowing only with the inside arm

PROBLEM	EFFECTS	POSSIBLE CAUSES
Missed oar stroke (oar-blades too far away from the water)	Too short a stroke in front of the gate, forward driving force too weak	Insufficient flexibility in the shoulders, height of the rigger, position of the hands and head
Arms bent too early	Forearms cramp, body leans too shortly forward, ineffective use of arms causing fatigue	(Stiff) upper part of body too upright, hands in wrong position, lack of balance when leaning forward
Premature use of upper trunk	Favours vertical movement, ineffective use of strength due to neglect of leg muscles	Angle of stretcher too sharp, heels too high, missed oar-stroke (upper trunk straightened up), inboard too hard
"Bum-shoving"* (= pushing the legs and hips backwards before driving the oar through the water)	Ineffective transfer of strength, back complaints	Underdeveloped back muscles, position of head, inboard too hard, lack of ability to coordinate limbs

Table 16: Second principle: rapid latching onto the water by the oar and exertion of pressure   *See also p. 90.

Possible Remedies

1. Coaching in flexibility; relaxation.
2. Strengthening of the muscles under stress.
3. Verbal hints, e.g. on position of the head.
4. Check dimensions of the boat (inboard, stretcher, rigger and fittings).
5. Getting a feel for the rowing position by scraping the oars over the water up to the catch.
6. Rowing only with the inside arm.
7. Exaggerated movements, e.g. sliding both hands down the loom to the gate.
8. Have the crew row with a team that can row properly.

PROBLEM	EFFECTS	POSSIBLE REMEDIES
The upper body moves jerkily during the final pull on the oar	The boat pitches, causing movements that sap the rower's strength, rower pulls on oars at maximum strength several times during a stroke	Stretchers are mispositioned, strength lacking in arms, incorrect understanding of movement
Extreme straightening of the rower's body	Inboards lifted over the knee, upper body collapses after final pull on the oars, the boat rocks	Rigger (gates) too low, incorrect understanding of movement, spine too stiff
Extreme backward lean	Reduction of pressure on the oar, straightening of the upper body costs time and strength, the boat pitches	Incorrect understanding of movement, insecure balance in the first part of the oar-stroke, stretcher needs adjustment
The upper body jerks into the forward position	Oar stroke misses the water, the boat loses speed	Stretcher needs adjusting, the sliding-seat jerks to a stop, the upper body does not accompany the seat when it slides

Table 17: Third principle: minimising vertical movements

Possible Remedies

1. Correct the rower's understanding of movement through demonstration and explanation, e.g. with the use of videos of very good teams.
2. Check the adjustments of the boat and the stretcher.
3. Rowing without an oar (pitching to-and-fro).
4. Rowing with the seat fixed, then gradually using greater physical effort to make the seat slide.
5. Demonstrating movement with pictures, e.g. rowing like a cat.
6. Training in flexibility.
7. Alternatively making an oar stroke in the water, then missing a stroke through the air.
8. Row slowly with low stroke frequency from ten strokes/minute to a maximum of twenty strokes/minute.
9. Rowing with a squared blade using the inside arm and then the outside arm.
10. Rowing with the hands gripping the oar but 20–30 cm close to the gate.

PROBLEM	EFFECTS	POSSIBLE CAUSES
The oar-blade is used like a *saw*	Oars are used less effectively, lower arms become cramped	Height of rigger, angle of oar, quality of the oar, position of the hands, the arms are incorrectly coordinated
The legs push unevenly during each stroke	Uneven pressure during each stroke, oars are used less effectively, the rower may become tired more quickly	Adjustment of the stretcher, hip or leg muscles are not strong enough
The oar blade turns in the water	Braking effect, requiring extra effort, onset of fatigue, rower "catches a crab" with the oar	Stretcher too far forward in the bow, rigger set too low, incorrect understanding of move-ment, premature breaking off of the oar stroke
"Hands off": hands too slow or too fast	Speed peaks, braking effect when raising oar out of water, oar stroke broken off too soon	Lack of power at end stage of oar stroke, wrong instructions on how to move, lack of coordination
Jerky or uncoordinated use of inboards	Balancing problems, loss of speed, coordination problems within the team	In sculls: compare the height of the riggers, over-long strokes, lack of concentration

Table 18: Fourth principle: even speed and acceleration of oar-movements

Possible Remedies

1. Explanation of physical conditions.
2. Let the crew row with a good team.
3. Have the crew row with squared blades, including more rapid strokes.
4. Check the dimensions of the boat and the oars.
5. Give help with matters of rowing rhythm.
6. Use varying ratings over short periods, e.g. 16–22–18 strokes etc.

The Fifth Principle: Problems in Team Coordination

Problems in team coordination are caused mostly by individual technical errors. As a result, particular notice should be taken of the effects and possible causes.

Possible Remedies

1. Help with rhythm.
2. Compare video films of the team with those of very good teams.
3. Rowing interspersed with breaks
   a)   at the front stops, just before putting the blades into the water.
   b)   directly after lifting the oars out of the water, the hands should still be drawn into the body.
   c)   when the hands are in front of the knees, the upper body leans slightly forward and the legs still stretch.
4. Rowing with the eyes closed (the rower should *think of him/herself* as the oar).
5. Varying the rating without major work in the water.
6. Start rowing, then let the oars trail through the water after dropping them in. Pause with the oars in front to the knees, on command move the body forward rapidly and dig the oars quickly and furiously into the water.
8. Rowing with the seat fixed, extend first the final part, then gradually the whole, sliding movement in the boat.
9. Rowing with one arm, then the other.
10. Row long stretches of water together.
11. Speed-exercises in the boat.
12. Perform intensive endurance and competition-related training together.
13. Training in rhythm, sliding forward, and pulling through in a set ratio.
14. Frequent rowing with a squared blade.
15. Measure the boat at regular intervals.
16. Let parts of the crew row together, e.g. in fours and doubles.
17. Change oar-type, e.g. from a coxless IV to a quad etc.
18. Do not permit monotony, always vary the exercises.
19. Do not talk too much about technique. A few extensive endurance units are often enough to restore team coordination.

Training

1. Aspects of Training

The *concept of training* in competitive sport is not only seen in the context of goals. In recent times, *training* has also come to mean a conscious, i.e. regular and specific influence as part of certain objectives and stages of biological development on increasing, maintaining and also (controlled) reduction (e.g. in lessening competitive rowing) of physical performance. Here the symptoms of biological adaptation are brought about through systematically repeated movement stimuli, which, besides the signs of physical adaptation, also have effects on the sportsman's mental state and personality (e.g. will, motivation, well-being and willingness to perform).

Regular and specific *training*, regardless of which goals are being pursued, requires a certain guidance. This guidance orients itself to certain biological patterns which are valid for every level of performance, sex, age and type of sport.

Rowing distinguishes between five large areas of training goals and orientation with respect to:

- Target-groups
- Length of training
- Symptoms of physiological adaptation
- Procedure
- Forms of organisation and competition
- Training equipment and methods

1. Fitness training
2. Basic training
3. Competitive rowing
4. High performance rowing
5. Rehabilitative and compensatory training

I. PREVENTION – HEALTH – FITNESS

Age group	Groups
Everybody	Leisure sports people families, senior citizens, recreational rowers, Masters

Aims:
- Health
- Well-being
- Physical fitness
- Body experience, self-confidence
- Social contact, social activity
- Competition in the mass sports (long-distance running, rowing triathlons and other types of sport)

Procedure:
1. Opportunities for fitness in the broad/general sense
2. Forming groups
3. Integration in the club
4. Fitness training
5. Development of an awareness of health

Forms of organisation and competition:
- General rowing activities
- Day trips, rowing holidays
- Rowing excursions
- Rowing competitions
- Games
- Regattas (at second competition level, Masters, etc)
- Social activities

Table 19: A guide to prevention – health – fitness in rowing

II. BASIC TRAINING

Age group	Groups
about 13–18 years	Juniors interested in training and competition

Aims:
- Developing rowing technique and tactics
- Developing the ability and will to perform
- Special training of individual performance factors for competitive racing (e.g. strength, endurance)
- Visits to regattas and competitions
- Closer involvement in club activities

Procedure:
1. Training is aimed at achieving performance in competitive rowing.
2. Retention of as wide a range of forms of exercise as possible (training on land and other types of sport).
3. Varying training according to physical ability, and methods with regard to the special demands.
4. Orientation via other rowing-related activities and enabling participation.

Forms of organisation and competition:
- Training
- Regattas
- Mass sports
- Rowing excursions
- Club and social activities

Table 20: A guide to basic training in rowing

III. COMPETITIVE ROWING	
Age-group	**Groups**
18 – 50 +	Adults and Masters willing to train and take part in competitive rowing

Aims:
- Regular visits to regional competitions and regattas
- Development and retention of the economic aspects of rowing-related performance (input and output)
- Preparation for honorary activities in the club

Procedure:
1. Development of a broad performance base
2. Formation of groups
3. Involvementn in the club

Forms of organisation and competition:
- Training
- Regattas
- Long-distance rowing
- Rowing triathlons
- State championships
- Overseas regattas
- Rowing excursions
- Indoor events

Table 21: A guide to competitive rowing

IV. HIGH-PERFORMANCE TRAINING

Age-group	Groups
about 19–30 years	Promising competitive rowers who have completed basic rowing training

Aims:
- Increasing performance in respect of individual ability and international rowing requirements
- Development of special endurance
- Improvement of technique and tactics
- International rowing successes
- Involvement in the club and (state) rowing association

Procedure:
1. Varying training by dates, partial goals and marks of performance
2. Rowing-related training (up to 75% of all the training)
3. Competitions to achieve a specific goal and main competitions
4. Involvement in a cadre and selection system

Forms of organisation and competition:
- Training
- Regattas
- Performance tests
- National and international championships
- Training camps

Table 22: A guide to high-performance training

V. REHABILITATIVE/COMPENSATORY TRAINING

Age group	Aimed at
	Sports people who have suffered injuries, the physically disabled

Aims:
- Restoration of physical performance and ability to take part in life (e.g. after illnesses preventing movement and after injuries)
- Compensation for psychological and physical suffering
- Extension of the opportunities for the physically disabled to become mobile (e.g. the visually impaired and the blind)
- Closer involvement in the social environment and in the club

Procedure:
1. Definition of the limitation
2. The prognostic aim
3. Selection of the opportunities available
4. Establishing the amount of activity to be taken part in
5. Measuring success

Forms of organisation and competition:
- Special and general rowing
- Day and longer excursions
- Local rowing competitions for non-club members
- Trip achievement awards
- Participation in the club's social events and integration in club life

Table 23: A guide to rehabilitative/compensatory training

2. The Principles of Training

The Law of Load and Adaptation

An increase in performance, or the drop in performance due to old age, would be inconceivable were a regular *interruption* of a generally remaining physical balance not to take place. A biological law (the law of homoeostasis) says that the organism tends to retain the dynamic balance between its performance ability and the demands on its performance (its environment). This *interruption* of the healthy organism's balance requires certain minimum stimuli. These stimuli must exceed a certain *stimulus threshold* because insufficient stimuli have no effect, and too high a stimulus harms the organism.

The excessive stimulus manifests itself in the organism as *fatigue*, but brings about the restoration of the energy potential which has been exhausted by the metabolic processes, and restores the ability to function (*regeneration*).

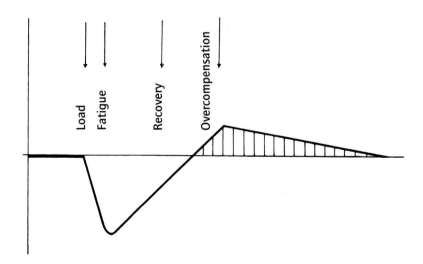

Figure 16: The law of overcompensation

Of course, training would be pointless if this adjustment did not take place over and above the original level (fig. 16). This increased balance or compensation, called *overcompensation*, loses its effectiveness again when the stimuli are not constantly repeated.

Training Frequency

As well as the correct amount of stimuli - *the intensity and length of the stimulus* - the frequency of training, i.e. the number of weekly load units, is also of considerable importance. In contrast to top sportsmen and women who wish to, or have to achieve maximum performance, the leisure sportsman or women has to think about a sensible relationship between cost and benefit. In general it is often more sensible to train for *shorter periods*, e.g. 4-5 times a week, than less frequently but for a longer duration, e.g. once a week for three hours. In rowing care should be taken that the load is of minimum duration:

1. Based on by how the training is organised (travelling time to the club, transport and care of the boats), training units of at least 30-45 minutes rowing-time are worthwhile.

2. Increased endurance needed for several and longer stretches, e.g. on a rowing excursion, cannot be so well-developed in units of under 30 minutes, since the corresponding physiological effect (metabolising of fats) does not begin until after this point.

As well, it is essential that the breaks between the load units are neither too long nor too short. If training is too infrequent or irregular, or if the recovery pause is too long, the *overcompensation* is reduced, and the trainees mark time. Stagnation or even a reduction in training condition can be caused by too short training breaks (*overtraining*).

The sensible exertion or training-frequency is determined by

- the sportsman's/-woman's current performance level.
- the type of load.
- the intensity of the load, its duration and volume.
- the quality of the recovery after the previous load.
- lifestyle (nutrition, sleep).

With top sports people, for example, this information on the determination of how training is designed and the optimising of the training plan is not sufficient. Sportsmen and women also use subjective feelings – called "listening to oneself" – in order to avoid overtaxing themselves. Leisure sportsmen and women also develop this ability in the case of deliberately designed training.

Increasing Exertion and Performance

An increase in performance has the effect of raising the stimulus threshold, from which the principle of increasing (progressive) load follows. If the same degree of load at the same intensity, same volume, is kept, the degree of load then appears less and the overcompensation diminishes. The load should therefore be increased every 2–3 months.

This increase in both the basics and high-performance training often takes place in leaps and bounds, and with the use of many types of training methods and equipment. In the area of fitness, a gradual increase in load is sufficient to avoid a stagnation or decline in performance.

Here attempts are made – taking into consideration the opportunities available to the sportsperson, of course – to pursue the following series of increases in loadin rowing (with the main aim of endurance):

1. Frequency of training
2. Volume of training
3. Number of stimuli
4. Intensity and length of stimuli
5. The intensity of load.

The better the physical condition,

• the less the increase in performance in relation to the effort put into training.

• the higher the effort made in order to retain this level of training.

Those who have not trained thus attain a high level of performance and fitness with little effort in a relatively short time. For the highly trained the relationship between effort and result becomes more and more uneconomic.

The Quality of Adjustment

Beside the condition factors for training, a kind of stress stimuli play an essential role for training efficiency. Special stimuli lead to special adjustment, i.e. the same quality of training (indicated by intensity, duration, volume, density, stimuli and frequency) but different compositions of training components lead to varying results. For example, fatigue can be caused by relatively brief but intense stimuli with defined breaks, exactly the same way that a less intensive but long stimulus can cause training effects of varying quality.

3. Loading Factors in Rowing Training

In training methodology the distinction between *external* and *internal* load has proved helpful. External load is laid down through load parameters, e.g. rowing for 20 km with a stroke-rate (SR) of 25-26 strokes/minute, with four bouts of seven minutes with an SR of 29-30 strokes/minute and a five minute break inbetween. The internal load describes the individual adjustment reaction, the degree of exertion that the individual sportsperson experiences at any given defined external effort. Rowers of different performance levels find the above training directions very stressful to various degrees, so that another adjustment reaction and therefore another training result can be expected apart from the degree of load (see fig. 17).

The structure of external load in rowing is characterised by the following components:

Load components	Quantification
Training frequency	Number of training units/week
Volume of training	km/minute, duration of training
Intensity	metres/second, metre/minute, stroke-rate
Duration of stimulus	sec., min., repetitions per series
Stimulus frequency	Number of individual stimuli
Density	Time-based relationship of load andrecovery, intervals between individual stimuli in a training unit

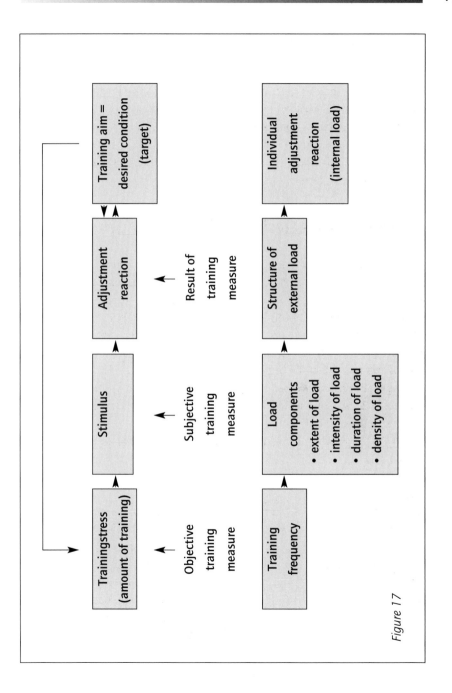

Figure 17

The desired adjustment reactions are only useful when based on internal load, especially where intensity is concerned. This is why physiological and biochemical data in high-performance rowing are obtained by load tests, which are then used as the basis for planning training and thus take into account current performance capacity or individual control. But the leisure and fitness area can also benefit, even if such costly and special procedures are rarely possible.

4. Intensity and Energy Supply

To further understand the connection of intensity, especially of internal load and design of training, a few remarks on physiology are necessary.

In order to move a boat through the water as quickly as possible, the rower needs energy which he obtains through the processes of chemical transformation in his muscle fibres. Energy-providing substrates are available for the transformation of chemically–linked energy, i.e. sugar in the blood, in mechanical form as glycogen (the form in which carbohydrates are stored) and as fats.

The very energy-rich adenosintriphosphate (ATP), which is stored in the muscles in very small quantities and suffices only for a few seconds or muscle contractions, provides this energy, which must be replaced constantly. This replacement takes place more or less in three interlocking steps (see figure 18):

1. For a period of about 10-15 seconds the stored creatine phosphate is used to produce ATP. This source of energy is for top performance lasting only a very short period.

2. The next source of energy is tapped when the stored glycogen in the muscle cells is used up *without* using oxygen (*anaerobic glycolysis*) during the formation of ATP and lactic acid (lactate).
   This energy source is easily available, but has the disadvantage that a lot of glycogen is required for the necessary transformation into ATP, and that lactic acid is formed as a *waste product*. In certain minimum concentrations lactic acid leads to an overacidification of the muscles, causing muscle fatigue.

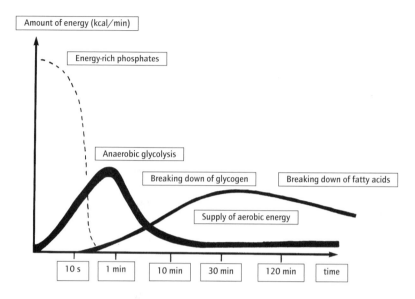

Figure 18: Energy supply varies according to the length of *load*

3. After a load lasting about 30 seconds the aerobic processes (oxydation) begin. With the help of oxygen, carbohydrates and fats are burned and the ATP is produced far more economically than by glycolysis.

Depending on the duration of the load, both energy sources, which are developed in their use and economy through training, are of immediate importance.

In rowing the aerobic processes are more important, but in competitive rowing anaerobic capacity can partly make up for the aerobic parts as well as be very important at certain stages of the race, e.g. the start and the final spurt at the finish-line. Aerobic and anaerobic energy production complement each other, but the amount of each varies according to duration, intensity and tactics of the particular form of exertion concerned.

One measure of whether reinforced aerobic and anaerobic exertion, i.e. the degree of internal exertion, is present, is the concentration of lactic acid in the blood. From these concentrations (which can be ascertained from blood in the ear lobes) up to about 2 mmol/l, a predominantly aerobic exertion can be deduced (the *aerobic threshold*). From more than 4 mmol/l of the anaerobic portion, predominantly anaerobic exertion can be deduced (*anaerobic threshold*). Up to this threshold most sportsmen succeed in maintaining performance over a long period of time. If concentration exceeds the threshold, it then increases very quickly in relation to the level of performance and leads to a rapid impairment in performance (figure 19).

A good sportsman trained for endurance sport only forms 2.5 mmol/l lactate in a given performance, but a less well-trained sportsman already has 8 mmol/l and is thus encumbered with higher quantity of anaerobes.

In order to determine endurance capability, the rowers performance is measured (e.g. on a rowing ergometer). The performance is given in watts at a lactic acid concentration of 4 mmol/l (the anaerobic threshold). This is normal practice and shows to some extent the rowers level of endurance, but not his maximum performance over 2,000 m.

Such readings are reserved mainly for high-performance rowers who train directly with the aid of various levels of load and allocation of heart-beat and concentration of lactic acid.

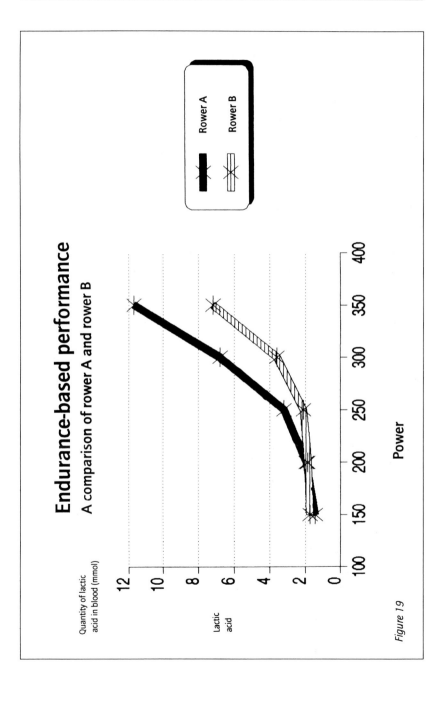

Endurance-based performance

A comparison of rower A and rower B

Quantity of lactic acid in blood (mmol)

Rower A

Rower B

Power

Figure 19

5. Areas of Increased Exertion in Rowing

To obtain the desired benefits from training, the rower should be aware of the following areas of increased load, or categories of load. As medical examinations and checks in performance are reserved only for top rowers, the placing of leisure rowers in these categories is made easier through further explanation.

Controlling *aerobic* performance and load is carried out mainly by increased activity in categories IV, V, VI. Overly frequent load over 4 mmol/l causes performance and physical development to stagnate – especially with up-and-coming rowers. Overly intensive and anaerobic load in those over the age of 40 and unfit can be dangerous. Those involved in rowing in order to keep fit choose load levels V and VI; those who wish to increase their physical fitness can – depending on age – train up to level III: the increase in lactic acid levels is accompanied by an increase in stress hormones and hence blood pressure. For this reason, high levels of load should remain preserved for top rowers and younger leisure rowers who are under medical supervision.

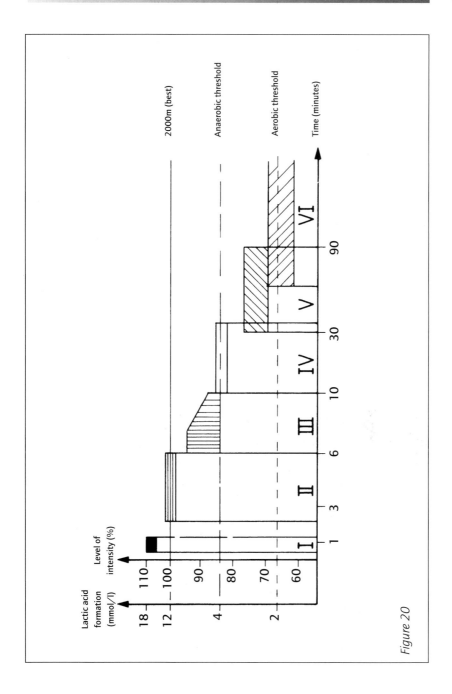

Figure 20

INTENSITY LEVEL I		
Objective	Starts and burns, speed, rowing technique at high stroke-rates	
Intensity	Lactate: at a stress of over 30 sec.: over 12 mmol/l, when rowing 2,000 m: 103–110%, Heart rate: > maximum of approx. 180 bpm	
Maximum period at this intensity	4–5 min/training unit	
Duration of individ. stimulus	a few seconds – 2 min	
Frequency/Breaks	2–15 min	
Energy supply	Up to approx. 15 sec.: Creatine phosphate (alactic), from 20 sec. upward: glycolysis (strong lactic)	
Subjective feeling	Highly motivated, maximum will to exertion necessary; extreme concentration, listlessness caused by difficulty in breathing and high concentrations of lactic acid	
Applications, aims	Fitness training:	—
	Training in the basics:	++ alactic 0 lactic
	Competition rowing and high-performance training:	++ alactic 0 lactic
	Recovery and compensation:	—
Examples:	*alactic:* 20 strokes (S) 1/2 slide, power, stroke frequency (SF) up to the maximum; increasing; starting exercises (up to 15 S) *lactic:* 4 x 30 S maximum from a standing start; 1 x 500 m maximum for a given length of time	

Explanation of symbols

–	**Pointless. Avoid.**
0	**To be used rarely and with care.**
+	**Necessary, but to be used in measured amounts.**
++	**Important for frequent use.**
+++	**Essential, determines the category of performance.**

INTENSITY LEVEL II	
Objective	Getting a feel for racing speed; tactical skills, speed endurance, economy of technique at high levels of exertion; competition rowing
Intensity	Lactate: 8–16 mmol/l, Racing: 98–100% of the max. performance over 2,000 m, Heart rate: >maximum of app 180 bpm
Maximum extent of intensity	5–12min / training unit
Duration of each stimulus	1-6 min In special situations, e.g. races: 5.5 – 8.5 min
Frequency/Breaks	2–15 min
Energy supply	Glycolysis + oxydation (according to length) burning of carbohydrates
Subjective feeling	Max. individ. speed over length of course, high degree of motivation necessary great effort of will, feelings of listlessness
Applications, aims	Fitness training: – Basic training: ++ Competition and high-performance training: +++ Recovery and compensation: –
Examples	Competition-related exertion, 3 x 1,000 m against the clock; 6 x 2 min racing stroke-rate (RSF); 10 min SF change for 60 s RSF, 30 s SF 26; 4 x 4 min race-pace with burns; 12 x 1 min RSF, 1min break

INTENSITY LEVEL III	
Objective	Special endurance and a high degree of specific strength endurance, tactics, team coordination, willpower training, improving maximum oxygen intake
Intensity	Lactate: 5-8 mmol/l Racing: 85-95% Heart rate: approaching maximum VO_2 max: 90-100%
Maximum extent of intensity	20/40 min/training unit
Duration of individ. stimulus	3-10 min
Frequency/Breaks	3-10 min
Energy-supply	Glycolysis + oxidation Burning of carbohydrates
Subjective feeling	Restricted range of vision and reasoning-capacity, listlessness due to increasing concentrations of lactic acid, great effort of will, lack of attention to surroundings, high degree of concentration necessary, only scraps of conversation possible, accelerated breathing
Applications, aims	Fitness training: - (health) 0 (physical fitness in younger rowers) Basic training: ++ Competitive rowing and high-performance training: ++ Rehabilitation and compensation: -
Examples	3 x 7 min 2-6 s at RSF; 3 x 2,000 m with increasing SR, no wind-up at start; 2 x 12 min SF change every 30-60 sec SF 30-26; 6-8 x 3 min SF 30-32; 3 min break

INTENSITY LEVEL IV	
Objective	Training willpower, Strength endurance aerobic capacity, intensive endurance training, improving oxygen intake
Intensity	Lactic acid: 3–6 mmol/l, anaerobic threshold Competitive rowing: 80–85% Heart rate: approx. 190 bpm minus age VO2 max: 80–90% max.
Maximum extent of intensity Duration of individ. stimulus Frequency/Breaks	10–45 min/training unit 1–45 min 0–10 min
Energy supply	Oxydation Carbohydrate metabolism plus use of muscle glycogen
Subjective feeling	High degree of load, breathing starts to become difficult, conversation is greatly reduced, higher degree of willpower and concentration necessary, field of vision narrows somewhat, average speed during long-distance rowing
Applications, aims	Fitness training 0 (health as an interval stress of 1–2 minutes) + (physical fitness) Basic training: ++ Competition training: ++ High-performance training: +++ Recovery and compensation: – (recovery) 0 (compensation)
Examples	2 x 20 min at full speed; 30 SF-change 18–28 s; 3 x 3,000 m 4–8 s under RSF, 5 min break; 10 km against the clock at a set SF Fitness: 20–30 min change every minute. 20–26 s; 3 x 6 min increasing SF 20-22-24-25-26, 5 min break

INTENSITY LEVEL V	
Objective	Development of aerobic (basic) endurance, stabilisation and renewal of the same level of endurance Training of technique
Intensity	Lactate: 1.5–3 mmol/l, Racing/competition: 70–80%, Heart rate: 180 bpm minus age (e.g. 140 bpm for a 40-year-old) VO_2 max: 70–80%
Maximum extent of intensity	30–100 min/training unit
Duration of individ. stimulus	30–100 min
Frequency/Breaks	None
Energy-supply	Metabolism of fats or carbohydrates (depending on length of activity)
Subjective feeling	Accelerated breathing, speech still possible but only in short sentences, greater concentration, landscape and environment still perceived
Applications, aims	Fitness training: + (health) +++ (fitness) Basic training: +++ Competition and high-performance training: +++ Recovery and compensation: +
Examples	Steady state with about 10–18 s under racing-rate when racing, e.g. over 90 min at SF 20–23; depending on level of training, length and intensity training respectively (here the SF) varies; SF changes are possible, higher SF, e.g. over 30, only over a shorter period (i.e. alactic)

INTENSITY LEVEL VI	
Objective	Training and consolidation of technique, training of willpower, basic endurance (vegetative nervous system, capillarisation), improved fat metabolism
Intensity	Lactate: under 2 mmol/l Racing: 65–70%, Heart rate: 170 bpm minus age VO_2 max: 60–70%
Maximum extent of intensity	30 min – several hours/training unit
Duration of individ. stimulus	30 min – several hours
Frequency/Breaks	Not required
Energy supply	Metabolising of fats via oxidation
Subjective feeling	A certain feeling for speed, very pleasant, conversation quite possible, breathing and heart rate hardly noticeable, the rower notices his surroundings
Applications, aims	Fitness training: +++ Basic training: ++ Competition and high-performance training: + Recovery and compensation: +++
Examples	Distances of any length and stroke-rate (up to about 20), well-suited for technique games in the boat, lively day-trips, excursions for more able rowers. Exercises of much lesser intensity than those mentioned here are solely for the purposes of recovery and active recuperation as well as for learning how to categorise movement sequences. Nevertheless they still provide health benefits.

6. Supplementary Training

For leisure rowing as well as basic and high-performance rowing it is a good idea to have information on complementary training *on land*. For example, in performance training strength training is indispensible, but those who row for fitness can also benefit from it. Complementary training often offers a balance and a change, and increases training opportunities in general. The following paragraphs sketch out for rowers the basics of some beneficial exercises. For reasons of space this section cannot go into too much detail about individual exercises, but there is a lot of good, well-illustrated literature available on the subject.

Strength Training

Human beings require strength for every movement. The physical definition of force (= the product of mass and acceleration) necessarily includes endurance and speed, for example when *strength* is needed over a longer period for endurance (very high speeds over long distances). Strength is specific to the particular sport being carried out and is always a combination of many capabilities and manifestations (maximum strength, strength endurance, strength in the various groups of muscles, etc). In order to do justice to this problem in the following paragraphs, we need to understand strength as the ability to move a mass, e.g. one's own body, a boat or piece of equipment, and to resist through muscle contraction.

The outward manifestation of strength in rowing depends on the type of action, intensity of effort and duration of rowing. To be successful in top-class international rowing a rower needs to expend about 50-70 N of effort per stroke for about 240 strokes. A recreational rower needs only 15-25 N for serveral hours at a stretch. The less the resistance to be overcome, the more insignificant *maximum strength* becomes. This is the greatest possible force capable of exerting voluntary muscle contraction.

Maximum strength for most rowing activity is thus relatively insignificant. However, it is also the basis for *strength endurance*, which is very important in rowing and particularly in competitions. This is the ability to maintain feats of *strength for the duration* of the race and to delay the drop in performance due to fatigue for as long as possible.

The duration of exercise and the proportion of maximum strength expended measured as a percentage determine whether power endurance tends towards strength (maximum strength) or endurance. In rowing, power endurance is coupled with the production of anaerobic and aerobic energy over the distance of the race because the resistance is to some extent very great, and the duration of the exertion is high.

Accordingly, special power endurance training in rowing must take into consideration four components:

1. The degree of resistance
2. The rapidity of the use of strength
3. The frequency of the use of strength
4. The volume and the duration of the use of strength.

For this reason the features of maximum strength training, speed training and anaerobic endurance should also be borne in mind during special strength training, apart from strength endurance.

Power means the ability to carry out movements at high speed against resistance.

Maximum strength training has two objectives:

1. an increase in muscle diameter
2. the improvement of intramuscular coordination.

Both require high-to-maximum muscle tension; the former requires a long lasting stimulus during the contraction, the latter must be carried out at top speed while the muscles are tensed. Full exertion is only of benefit if carried out while the muscles are rested, and if there has been a sufficient period of recovery between each bout of load.

Within *power*, two forms of training relevant to competition rowing may be distinguished:

1. The abrupt overcoming of a high level of resistance, e.g. at the start of a race.

2. Rapid movements, which also help to improve coordination and require increased production of lactic energy, in contrast to training for maximum strength and the initial form of power training.

When carrying out *strength endurance training*, it should be remembered that the resistance to be overcome is higher than in a rowing race, for example, and that because of the load structure the muscles tire noticeably.

Outward form / Training effect	Intensity	Repetition Series	Breaks	How carried out
Maximum strength Cross-section enlargement	75-90%	6-10 3-5	2-4 min	quickly slowly
Maximum strength Intramuscular coordination	85-100%	1-5 3-5	2-5 min	abruptly quickly
Power High resistance	50-75%	6-10 4-6	2-4 min	abruptly
Power Speed, Coordination	46-60%	10-20 5-8	30-90 sec	fast
Strength endurance Can be set higher as a contest	40-60%	30-50 5-8	30-90 sec	fast

Table 24: Overview of the structure and methods of strength training

All forms and objectives of strength training can be carried out in rowing but, with the exception of strength endurance training, require a high level of ability in rowing technique. Even here the higher the performance level, the more specialised the strength training must be. This means that the training must take place in the boat in order to increase racing performance.

There are many means of strength training available. Carrying out this form of training depends, of course, to a large extent on the space and equipment available to the rower or the club:

1. Exercises without equipment, e.g. one's own weight, exercises with a partner or gymnastics.
2. Exercises with small items, e.g. medicine balls, sandbags, small handweights, weighted vests, etc.
3. Exercises with larger equipment, e.g. boat, larger weights, gymnastic equipment, benches, wall bars, gymnastic ropes and climbing poles.

Strength training on the leg-exerciser

The deciding factor in achieving the most benefit from training is not so much the choice of training equipment but the right amount of training.

Generally speaking, the more specialised a sportsman is, the less opportunity he has of using all the available training equipment to full advantage. Special rowing-related endurance and strength endurance can be developed to a very high level only by rowing itself or by movements that simulate rowing, e.g. on a rowing ergometer, weightlifting using movements that simulate rowing, training in the tank, etc. It is even questionable as to whether general power training with weights can increase general rowing performance without specific rowing-exercises at top-level. There is certainly a beneficial effect on general fitness.

Leisure rowers and would-be rowers doing basic training, on the other hand, can and should use the great variety of training equipment to full advantage, keeping in mind the desired load levels. Top rowers can do this, too, provided they want to increase their overall fitness.

Leisure and beginner rowers should not specialise in any one or more sorts of strengthening exercises too much when beginning basic rowing training. At this stage their main goal is to increase their general physical fitness; the central training goal remains endurance. A rower achieves general strengthening when the intensity of the exercises reaches 60–90% of maximum potential; exercises can be repeated from at least five to twelve times.

The exercises and resistances should be chosen correspondingly, because high numbers of repeats do not necessarily guarantee an increase in the diameter. These also produce too much lactate.

The improvement or maintenance of the diameter of the muscle requires high exercise intensity, which is why, when choosing exercises to increase general strength, it is best to avoid work above head or external load, for example, with partners or handweights.

As a rule the rower's own weight, or smaller equipment such as a medicine ball or a sandbag are enough but latterly more sophisticated equipment (such as that found in a fitness studio, for example) is also sufficient.

Special Forms of Strengthening Exercises for Rowing

1. Arms and shoulders
   - Various forms of pull-ups

   - Arm bends (bench-pulls)

- Press-ups (front and back)
- Lifting apparatus
- Working with leg-exercisers (pulling a band or a chain to exercise the legs)

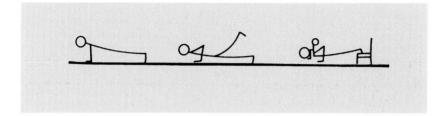

- Forearm curls with extra weights

- Arm-stretches (bench-presses etc)

- Weight-pulls (using the lower arms)

2. Legs and hips
   - Squat-jumps
   - Two footed squat-jumps
   - Leg press

- Squats with extra weights
- Step-ups with extra weights

3. Torso and back
  - Hyperextensions

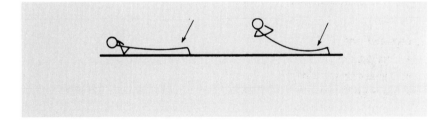

- Hyperextension (see above) but with a partner or on a bench (see photo p. 137)
- Leg-raises on a box with the trunk lying on the horse

- Side sit-ups.
- Raise one leg, then the other while lying on the belly.
- Throw a medicine ball backwards over head.

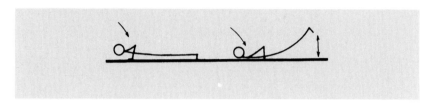

- Straightening the upper body from a forward bending position into an upright position while holding a weight.

4. The front side of the body
   - Lying on the back with the feet held down, raise the body into an upright position (sit-ups).

- Lie on the back and raise the legs, either together or one at a time.

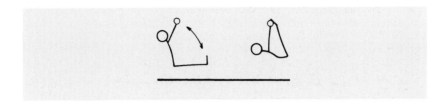

- While hanging on the wall bars, raise the legs over the head.

- As above, but move the legs sideways or just raise the knees.

- While lying on the back with the arms stretched out holding a weight-bar with weights, move the weights over the head backwards until the weights sit on the floor. Then bring them back again over the chest as if throwing in a soccer ball in slow motion, and lower them onto the chest.

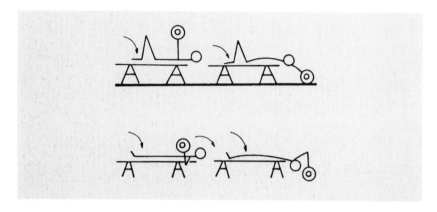

Bench-press

Pull-over exercise

Hyperextension with a partner or on a bench (see p. 133)

- Throw-in the medicine ball.
- Lying on the back on a bench with the arms stretched out sideways, bring the arms back over the rib-cage ("butterfly" exercise).
- With a partner: pull the partner over the shoulders or back.

5. Exercises for the whole body
  - Assume the press-up position. Without moving the hands, bring the legs up to a crouch position, then quickly straighten the legs out and resume the push-up position (combined squat thrusts).
  - Stretch-jump on the horizontal bar, finishing off with a pull-up.
  - Jerk-ups with the weight-bar.

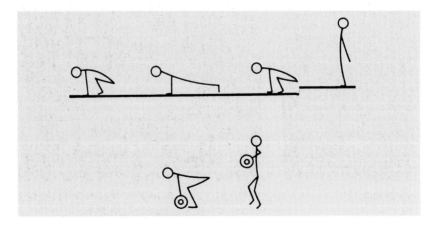

- Lifting dumbbells off the floor and over the head.
- Special apparatus simulating rowing movements.
- Rowing ergometer or windwheel.
- Rowing tank.
- Squats while lifting the arms holding weights. Special exercise (see photo below).
- Jerks (weight-lifting using sudden, jerking movements).

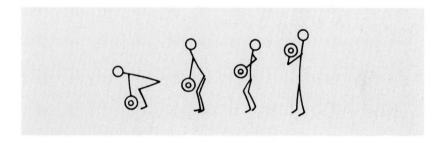

Special exercise

Bench-pulls (lifting weights lying on the belly on a bench and pulling weights up off the floor)

Flexibility

The ability to perform movements within a large radius at will is called flexibility. In rowing a high degree of flexibility is required in the shoulders, spine and hips. Flexibility as a performance-inhibiting factor in rowing does not always receive the recognition it deserves, although it can fulfill the following important functions:

- avoidance of injuries
- enabling an economy of movements
- making easier the acquisition of movements
- having a positive effect on strength, speed and endurance.

For general flexibility training, about ten repetitions of an exercise are enough (done 2-3 times a week), which can be increased in intensity after every five repetitions. The intensity of the stretching stimulus is very high, i.e. it is close to pain level. Apart from general physical condition, it depends on:

- age
- time of day
- level of fatigue
- anatomical condition, i.e. the condition of the limbs
- clothing
- warm-up
- temperature
- rower's mental state.

Flexibility training is mostly applied in conjunction with other performance factors; however, it is important that it is carried out at the proper place in the training session. It makes most sense to perform flexibility training *after* the warm-up and *before* more strenuous exercises.

Flexibility is usually associated with "gymnastics". Taking into account the increase in intensity of the exercises, these should be carried out *systematically from the head to the feet*, broken up by loosening-up exercises, and can be performed several times at various levels of intensity.

Apart from *active* stretching, one way of increasing the level of intensity is *passive* stretching. With the help of a partner, the rower can perform movements in a wider range than in active stretching exercises. Teenagers under 15 and older rowers should take care when performing passive flexibility exercises.

Some exercises for rowing (without equipment)

- With the palms of the hands touch the floor with the legs straightened.
- To increase the level of difficulty, stand on a bench and bring the hands down as far as they will go.
- Spread the legs, straighten the knees and, with the hands, reach between the legs to the rear.
- Straighten the knees and try to touch one, then the other, with the head.
- Assume a sideways straddle position. Then touch the left ankle with the left hand and the right ankle with the right hand alternately. Do not lean forwards or backwards.
- Lying on the back, try to put the legs as far as possible behind the head without straightening the knees.
- Kneel down, put the elbows back with the head leaned back.
- Go down onto one knee, raise the arms and lean back.

Flexibility exercises performed as circuit training
(can be done in a gym)

1. Shoulders: using stretched out arms, a pole is brought from behind to the front of the trunk of the body. The rower's degree of flexibility determines how the pole is held.
2. Spine: keeping the feet in the same position on the floor, the rower rotates rings around the straightened body.
3. Sides of the body: lying on his belly the rower stretches out his right foot and tries to touch it with the right hand. He then tries the same with the left arm and left leg.
4. Spine, back: the rower stretches out on the floor and tries to turn on his own axis without his arms or legs touching the floor.
5. Hips, backs of the legs: the rower stretches one leg, then the other, over a box.
6. The adductor muscles: the rower puts his feet inside rings, holds onto the rope and stretches his adductor muscles longways and sideways.

Complementary Sports Promote Endurance

While rowing cultivates all forms of endurance extremely well, it is advisable to complement training with the help of other sports that promote endurance. This helps physical fitness for both the leisure rower and the high-performance rower.

These sports:
- promote psychological relaxation and relief
- enable a relatively large transfer (adaptation of the vegetative nervous system, economy in the cardio-vascular system and metabolism) at a low level of physical activity
- extend the fitness programme and make a welcome change
- present an alternative to outside training when the weather is bad, e.g. heavy seas, when water is very cloppy, when streamis too strong, when the river or lake is iced over or when the weather is cold.

The type of load of exercises correspond in intensity and comprehensiveness to that of rowing training (see the chapter on "Training"). However the various advantages and disadvantages should also be borne in mind.

Overview of Complementary Sports Promoting Endurance

1. Rowing ergometer and windwheel	
Transferability (to rowing):	Very high
Area of intensity (recommended):	Category VI-III
Duration (recommended):	20–80 min
Advantages:	Precise amounts, almost equivalent to practice under racing conditions, can be carried out in all weathers, lends itself to competitions
Disadvantages	Large room needed for practice (oxygen), boring (can only be put up with when listening to music)

2. Cross-country skiing

Transferability:	High
Area of intensity:	Category VI-III
Duration:	45 min – several hours

Advantages:	Exercises the whole body, relatively little stress on joints good training opportunity during winter holidays, races for non-competitive rowers, can be practiced outside in the open countryside, can be practiced as a hike
Disadvantages:	Snow and cross-country trails necessary, obtaining equipment and clothing cost money, weather-dependent, movements usually have to be relearned

3. Cycling

Transferability:	Average
Intensity:	Category VI-IV
Duration:	30 min – several hours

Advantages:	Little stress on joints, enables cycling tours, can be undertaken immediately without too much expense (one can start at one's own front door)
Disadvantages:	Other traffic on the road, danger of accidents, equipment (bicycle) necessary

4. Swimming

Transferability:	Average
Intensity:	Category V-III
Duration:	20–60 min
Advantages:	Whole body receives exercise, little stress on joints; relatively high level of physical strength required, physical stimuli
Disadvantages:	Technical skills necessary, muscles tire quickly if out of practice, danger of infection, overly full swimming-pools

5. Running

Transferability:	Fair to average
Intensity:	Category IV-VI
Duration:	15–90 min
Advantages:	Can be performed at any time and almost anywhere; competition possible at all levels; needs no special equipment
Disadvantages:	Danger of injury, damage to joints (feet and knees)

6. Circuit training for endurance

Transferability:	Average to high exercises
Intensity:	Category IV-III
Duration:	20–60 min
Advantages:	Training groups easily observable. can be practised in spite of weather, by choosing the right exercises, specific muscles can be exercised
Disadvantages:	Difficult to measure the right number of exercises, more suitable for intensive endurance training

7. In-line Skating	
Transferability:	Average
Intensity:	Category V-VI
Duration:	15 min – several hours
Advantages:	Little stress on joints, skater can cover long distances
Disadvantages:	Danger of injuries for beginners, costs for equipment and accessories, cannot be performed everywhere

7. Recovery

After each kind of training session the rower needs corresponding recovery periods. Recovery is basically influenced by the following factors:

- Training age
- Age and sex of the rower
- Type of load, e.g. strength endurance, speed
- Content of previous training units
- Intensity and extent of load
- The psychological state of the rower
- The rower's nutrition and lifestyle
- The use of any (physio-) therapeutic treatment
- Stress at work or in relations with other people.

Thus, while a training unit may have contained an optimal load, the rower may find the same stress a few days later too great, for example, due to job-related demands. If the load is set too high, or the recovery time too short, a rower may end up being *overtrained*, and the rower's performance drops noticeably. Should the recovery not yet be complete, the following training units must be of a recuperative nature.

Depending of the various types of training loads, the recovery times are set out as follows:

Type of exertion	Rapid recovery (in hrs)	Slow recovery (in hrs)
Aerobic endurance VI	–	–
Aerobic endurance V	–	12
Aerobic endurance IV	1,5 – 2	24 – 36
Aerobic/anaerobic (mixed)	2 – 3	24 – 28
Anaerobic-lactic	2 – 3	48 – 72
Anaerobic-alactic	2 – 3	–
Maximum strength	2 – 3	72 – 84

In the recovery process there is a distinction made between a quick and a slow recovery. The quick one requires approximately 1 1/2-hours. During this period the superfluous acidification in the muscles is removed, the liquid and mineral content is brought back to normal and most of the glycogen is replenished.

Only the slow recovery fully replenishes the glycogen supply (this takes up to three days). In young people especially, the vegetative nervous system usually requires more than 3–4 days for complete recovery.

Measures which may support recovery are:

1. Nutrition
   - reducing stimulants, e.g. caffeine
   - reducing alcohol consumption, preferably cutting it out completely
   - eating vitamin-rich foods
   - eating mostly fruit and vegetables.

2. Physical and climatic measures

- Massages
- Swimming in heated swimming pools
- Swimming in open-air swimming pools
- A change of climate, e.g. going for walks in the country or particularly hill walking.

3. Rest and Relaxation

- Sufficient sleep
- A lifestyle appropriate to sporting activity
- A sports-friendly environment.

As a rule the above exercises are part of training for those rowers active in competitive sport. From the point of view of training structure and methods they can contribute to a quicker recovery on the part of the rower. This affects the series of training units which relies on the prime energy-producing methods:

After	Alactic load (I)	Lactic load (II; III)	Intensive aerobic load (IV)	Extensive aerobic load (V; VI)
the following are recommended:				
Alactic load	–	–	+	++
Lactic load	–	–	–	++
Intensive aerobic load	+	–	–	+
Extensive aerobic load	++	++	++	–
Key to symbols:	– = avoid	+ = possible	++ = a good idea	

Table 25

PART 3: ROWING IN DAILY LIFE

Fitness and Well-being in Rowing

The concept of *fitness* comes up in many contexts. Apart from physical and neuro-locomotor considerations, psychological and social elements also play a role. Each individual sets his/her own emphasis according to his/her own values and motivation.

Sport in general can also offer several options for getting or staying fit. Although in rowing each component can be developed on its own, in this sport in particular they are linked to a large extent. If all aspects of fitness are regarded as equal, the following "concepts" may be offered:

1. Fitness as a means of preventing illness and slowing down the ageing process (health).
2. Fitness as a means of maintaining or increasing physical performance (physical fitness).
3. Fitness as a means of achieving physical and psychological recovery, self-realisation through pleasure, endeavour and relaxation in sports activities (well-being).
4. Fitness as a successful means of contact with one's environment, achieving recognition and cooperation with others (social skills).

1. Rowing and Health

The importance of physical movement as a means of achieving optimal physical development is undisputed.

As human beings are in increasing danger from this world of high technology, the fact that physical characteristics such as strength, endurance and flexibility continue to regress means that they must deliberately engage in movement and physical exertion to compensate for this. Symptoms of a lack of movement manifest themselves chiefly in very common ways:

- Cardiovascular diseases
- Ailments and malfunctions of the vegetative nervous system
- Weakness in, and damage to, posture
- Obesity.

In order to prevent degeneration, the body requires certain stimuli. Those people not engaging in physical exertion become weaker over a long period of time and, sooner or later, suffer the harmful effects of modern life. Since these stimuli hardly appear in everyday life, they must be presented during leisure time in the form of sport.

Leisure activities such as rowing help to prevent the symptoms of a lack of exercise, thus contributing to the health of the individual. They:

- prevent cardiovascular damage through exercises in aerobic endurance (basic endurance).

- improve the ability of the vegetative nervous system to adjust, for example between different loads, outdoor rowing all year round and in all types of weather

- prevent muscular atrophy and posture problems by exercising muscles through rowing; all the major muscle groups are involved in the rowing movement, especially those in the trunk and the upper body

- prevent diminishing flexibility and tension by stretching and moving the spine and the shoulders

- prevent obesity by the particularly high and measured burning of calories.

The special advantage of rowing as a *health-promoting sport* consists of exercising and developing all organs equally; the risk of injury is also very slight.

2. Rowing and Physical Fitness

Rowing is an excellent way of reaching a generally high standard of physical fitness in order to cope more easily with the demands of everyday life, for example at work or in order to increase one's performance in other sports.

A good standard of physical fitness is characterised by the high, even standard of development of all the elements of the rower's physical fitness (strength, endurance, speed, flexibility). Training these abilities conforms to biological laws of adaptation for the improvement or maintaining of physical performance. Rowing, performed according to these laws, is thus particularly suitable as fitness training because it:

- improves the general and specific elements of fitness such as strength, endurance, speed and flexibility.

- increases the ability of the muscles to resist injuries.

- avoids illnesses of the internal organs.

- improves general and specific coordination (skill, dexterity, muscular control).

3. Rowing and Well-being

Rowing provides a direct physical experience: exertion – up to the limits of each individual's physical capacity, e.g. in a rowing race, fatigue after a long day-stretch of a rowing expedition, relaxation and rest in the country.

It is difficult to relax and rest by means of sport without subjecting oneself to great physical effort. At the same time a certain degree of regularity and level of skill do appear to be necessary, as only this regularity and repeated practice promote enjoyment and pleasure in rowing.

This type of fitness transcends the area of physical and health aspects and aims at the area of self-awareness, the effects of which one only becomes aware of after experiencing them personally.

4. Rowing and Social Life

Rowing is a team sport and hence, to a large extent, a social sport.

Besides the team influence, rowing is connected with club life in a special way. Socialising as a type of "social fitness" derives its existence from the individual's contact with his social environment, recognition from and cooperation with, others.

- Rowing in established teams or groups develops and passes on a feeling of belonging; one is forced into contact, and to get along with others.

- Team members can socialise while rowing. Each rower can experience being part of a group.

- Rowing offers many sorts of opportunities for socialising, whether functions put on by the club, (naming a new boat, rowing club dances etc.) or smaller and less formal forms of socialising such as a regulars' table at the local pub, club meetings, etc.

Fitness training thus pursues many aims and emphases. Good fitness training, and this goes for all fitness programmes carried out with any intensity, should, of course, primarily be fun. Only when these individual elements are combined do they become fully effective. Rowing combines these elements extremely well, but a few tips should also be observed.

5. Medical Checks and Common Sense

Everybody who has decided to take part in a fitness programme, regardless of volume or intensity, should first have a thorough medical examination to make sure that there is no ailment preventing the necessary exertion intended in the programme. Even rowers who have performed very well in races in past years and then had to give up for several years or in some cases for several decades, for job-related or other reasons, should protect themselves from any injuries caused by getting back into rowing.

While they have the advantage of still knowing how to row, their performance will have decreased physiologically. Such people run the great danger of over-exerting themselves after taking up rowing again.

The nature of rowing is such that rowers will always be on the water for a long time. As a rule one should plan for training units lasting 60–70 minutes. Given this amount of time, it is all the more important to choose exercises of the appropriate intensity and not be afraid of having a rest.

As a lifetime sport, rowing offers people of all age groups the opportunity to improve or maintain their level of personal fitness. As a rule, peoples' sporting performance peaks before 30 years of age. After that it decreases due to age, but once a certain level has been reached it can be maintained for a longer period (or performance decreases at a slower rate) if certain pointers are followed:

After the age of 40 performance generally takes a decided dive. Rowing training prevents the drop in physiological performance and has a positive effect on the performance of the organs, not only of those who have been doing sport on a regular basis but also of non-sportsmen and newcomers to rowing.

For those over 50 rowing serves primarily to maintain performance and health. The age-determined decrease in the capacity of the cardiovascular system can often be considerably slowed by means of general cardiovascular endurance training. With the exception of breathing (solely by economy in breathing), circulation and metabolism can be improved.

If somebody has rowed regularly for many years, it is possible to maintain performance even into one's 60's by observing the following points:

1. No maximum performance in advanced old age.

2. In cases of arteriosclerosis and high blood pressure, training with high levels of pressure is neither safe nor advisable.

3. Rowing should be continued without great differences in exertion (variations of intensity).

These pointers serve not only as health tips but also to promote leisure rowing in groups for those of different ages, sexes and abilities.

6. Forms of Competition for Leisure Rowers

Regattas

The alteration of the classical competition course from 2000 m downwards (to 500 m, 1000 m or 1500 m) and upwards (long-distance courses between 4 km and 150 km) shows a desire to take the wishes of rowers on various levels of performance for organised forms of competition, into account.

Rowing Rallies and Orienteering on the Water

The authors HELD and KREISS developed rowing rallies and orienteering on the water for sports with large numbers of participants. These activities are both a game and a competition, and are highly suitable for certain rowing areas such as lakes.

The Rowing Rally

The teams are given photos or descriptions of certain places (towns, buildings, landscapes) and are "started" at given time intervals in order to look for these places. At the finish-line points are given for the correct number of places found.

Orienteering on the Water

Similar to orienteering on foot, the teams have to row to hidden checkpoints on the banks of a river with the help of a map. At these checkpoints there are various tasks to be carried out either individually or in groups. The order in which the rowing teams row to each checkpoint can be determined by each team. Points are given for solving the tasks and the time in which the whole course is completed.

Open Rowing; Rowing Marathons

Individual clubs arrange these events in order to compete with other neighbouring clubs according to their own ability in their own way:
The organisers award gold (30 km), silver (20 km) or bronze (10 km) medals for races with any sorts of boats and teams of all sorts of competitors. These events are not timed. Apart from these sports activities there are opportunities for a social get-together for club members and people from other clubs.

Long Distance Races

Originally meant for competitive rowers, long distance races also enjoy increasing popularity and are catching on more and more with leisure rowers and Masters.
This is due mainly to the fact that these races are carried out in racing boats – frequently as sculling races – but also in team boats.

Ergometer Competitions (Indoor Rowing)

Indoor rowing is enjoying enormous popularity. Here, innumerable events are offered in winter as an alternative to the racing season for those of all ages and abilities and, of late, in the German Championships.

The development of ergometers has progressed further, and those used for everyday training have become relatively inexpensive. This has led not only to more of such equipment being made available by clubs but also to many rowers obtaining their own "ergo" as a "home trainer".

The easy comparison and measurability of performance among rowers makes these ergometers important, not only as a physiological performance-testing device in top-class rowing, but also gives leisure rowers an objective idea of their physiological development.

The Rowing Triathlon

The rowing triathlon is an increasingly popular variation of rowing and is attracting great interest.

Instead of including swimming in the triathlon, many variations of rowing are included. In accordance to the wishes of the organisers and the performance and age of the participants, the courses are between 20 km and 120 km in overall length. This is divided up into partial disciplines as follows:

a. Rowing: 20–10 km (lower limit 4.5 km)
b. Cycling: 80–25 km (lower limit 10.5 km)
c. Running: 20–5 km

A rowing triathlon is particularly exciting as a team competition. The following options are possible as a team effort:

- After the team rowing, cycling and running have been carried out as a unit, the rowing triathlon as a real team effort is assessed.

- After the team rowing, the fourth member of a team of five gets points for the time taken in the other disciplines.

- The individual performance of all rowers assessed as a team is added up.

- A triathlon can be carried out in a pairs: rowing in a coxless pair, riding a tandem bicycle and running as a team.

It is hoped that this new form of rowing competition increases in as many variations as possible and constitutes an option for all ages and abilities.

Rowing Trips

One special and distinct form of rowing as a popular sport is in the form of a rowing trip. Rowing trips have a long tradition and are one of the central elements of rowing and its attractions.

Enjoying the countryside, travelling along familiar or unknown waters, and group trips require certain minimum levels of physical fitness in order to manage stretches of 30–50 km or more each day. The degree and the specifics of physical fitness depend here on the length and the conditions of each leg, either for that day or for the whole journey.

1. Various Forms of Rowing Trips

One way of differentiating between the various forms of rowing trips is their duration. On a *day-trip*, participants row to a given destination from which they row back to the club or are picked up by other club members, who bring the boat back to the club on the trailer.

Day-trips of about 25-60 km in length can fulfill several tasks:

- A club trip to a neighbouring club
- Consolidating rowing technique for advanced beginners.
- Getting used to and preparing for longer trips, e.g. trips of several days in length.
- Family trips.

Another favourite form of rowing trip is the *weekend trip*. Rowers require a higher level of physical fitness in order to take the increased load over two or three days and a distance of 50-80 km. This assumes earlier practice trips of some length or even several day-trips.

Besides practice in technique and adequate physical condition, the rower should have mastered steering. Such trips are particularly attractive for young people, as they can camp out over night.

The most attractive form of rowing trip is the *rowing holiday* or *longer rowing excursion*. These can last from several days to several weeks and require thorough preparation and an experienced trip leader. In such instances the participants must know how to use the equipment and how to cope with specific situations.

An excursion of several days' length also requires special endurance and the ability to take physical strain. Generally, it also presumes that the rower has taken part in several day-trips before, and physical fitness training. On very long excursions (from 7-10 days) it is a good idea to plan extra days and rest days into the trip.

The tasks of such trips are as varied as the needs of the participants. Some want healthy rest and recuperation (R & R) in the country, some want culture and a good time with others. Some want to cover 2,000 km with others on a voyage of discovery, and to be able to say that they have been on a river that nobody - or hardly anybody - has been on before. For a few people rowing excursions become a sort of competitive sport and they are proud of having rowed from Basle to Cologne. A rowing excursion can easily be combined with other sporting activities as well. More and more popular with young people are combined rowing-biking tours with either mountain or touring bikes.

The attraction here is the change of perspective: one sees and experiences the landscape from a different point of view. Besides being able to carry out one sport parallel to another, the participants have the opportunity of combining a rowing trip with a cycle tour. Instead of cycling beside the boat, the participants can explore the countryside around the stretch being travelled through or around the destination by bicycle. This also combines the interests of participants of various ages and abilities very well.

2. Preparing for a Rowing Trip

The first stage in planning a rowing trip is to establish the participants' wishes and needs, so that the planning and executing of the trip can proceed successfully.

Rowing excursions require preparations to be made a very long time in advance, especially when assistance and information in organisational matters is needed from others, e.g. boats, team transport, accommodation, unknown waters. During the planning stage the following points should be taken into consideration:

The Composition of the Group and the Objectives of the Participants

Homogeneous groups	• Young people • Former members • Ladies' excursions • Former competitive rowers
Heterogeneous groups	• Men and women • People of different ages • People of different abilities
Importance:	• Type and cost of accommodation and food • Length of the course and the conditions (risk) • Cultural amenities along the way • The importance of natural beauty • Transport available to the participants and boats • Insurance, supervisory and legal matters

Sources of Information

Comparing notes
- Among those who take part in rowing trips
- Between rowing clubs

Literature
- The Rowing Almanac of the National Rowing Association or Federation
- A manual for rowing excursionists
- Reports from rowing-related periodicals
- Travel literature

Addresses
- Clubs (canoeing and rowing)
- Associations
- Waterways authorities

Materials
- Brochures and leaflets from tourist agencies
- Maps
- Rowing Association announcements

Choice of the Route

Duration of the excursion
- Length of the trip and back from the destination
- Team transport
- The degree of difficulty of the route
- The season
- Length of general and public holidays

The condition of the route
- The beauty of the landscape
- Other boat traffic; locks
- Cultural events
- Accommodation
- Conditions on the water, including the weather

Organisation
- Club boats or borrowed boats (costs)
- Transport of the boats
- Division of the route into individual legs
- Accompanying vehicle

Equipment

Boats
- Suitability for special routes
- Suitability for participants (weight)
- Sculling boats or rowing boats

Accessories	• Floorboards
	• Rudder
	• Flag
	• Boathook
	• Spare gates and lines
	• Life jackets
	• Repair equipment, spare boat parts
	• First aid kit
Personal items	• Sufficient t-shirts and rowing shorts, swimwear, training suits, rain gear
	• Sleeping bag, groundsheet
	• Toiletries, toilet paper
	• Sun protection (hat, cap, lotion)
	• Money bag, money, ID (if applicable)
	• Tourist guidebook, maps, torch
	• Camera

Insurance

By the participants	• Medical, accident, liability
	• Luggage?
By the club	• Boat transport
	• Liability (for borrowed boats and for others encountered on the water)

Other

- Right-of-way on the waters to be rowed on
- Locks (lengths, how they work, opening times)
- Clubs, opportunities for accommodation
- Parents' permission for minors
- Information for the participants about conditions on the waters to be travelled on, and necessary abilities and skills
- Post-trip arrangements: return of equipment, paying bills, post-trip get-together

3. Going on a Rowing Trip

Manning the Boats; Stowing Luggage

The trip leader appoints a head rower for every boat and sees to it that all boats are more or less equally manned in terms of efficiency, so that the gaps between each leg of the route do not become too great and that the waiting periods are limited. The participants should be instructed to take their hand luggage to their seat in the boat and store it there. This prevents any rummaging through the well- stowed, equally distributed luggage in the bow and stern of the boat. Hand luggage should be tied firmly to the crossribs and, apart from food and drink for the trip, includes sun protection and rain gear, cameras, a guidebook of the river, an ID (if applicable) and money.

Entering and Leaving a Lock

The participants should be told in advance how locks work. They are always a source of danger for people and property and for this reason extreme care and discipline are required. A boat-hook is an absolute must; two hooks per boat are even better. The rowers let the current float the boat into the *lock* with the oars pulled up and held parallel to the boat by the hands. There are markings on the insides of the lock showing the positions the boat is to be held. When travelling downstream the boat should always be held at the stern (and at the bow as well, if possible) with the ladder intended for this purpose. When travelling upstream, the boat should be held by the bow. Extreme care should be taken to ensure that any rig is not caught in the protrusions on the walls of the lock. A special form of lock for boats are those combined with a fish* steps. In these locks the boat should sail as closely as possible to the far end of the lock.

In locks designed for *larger boats*, care should be taken that rowing boats always enter behind motorboats and tie up behind them. As a rule the lock-keeper will give a signal to do this. Special care is necessary when the motorboat in front starts its motor before leaving the lock. Quite often the resulting wash will rock the boat back and forth, thereby swamping it.

---

* *Fish steps are sets of steps permitting fish to migrate past weirs and locks when making their way upstream to breed.*

A rowing trip on the Saar River

What to Do If the Boat Is Swamped

It only takes the wash of a passing motorboat or heavy seas to cause problems for a rowboat: water is often washed over the gunwale or the rigger. When waves get white caps on them due to high winds, the trip should be broken off and the crew should make for the nearest land and tie up there. Even small amounts of water in the boat should be baled out with plastic containers or sponges etc.

If a boat is swamped in strong winds or in the wake of a passing boat and it is impossible to go on rowing, the crew should get out and swim to the bank, pushing the boat with them. An iron rule here is: all crew members must stay with the boat! Loose pieces of luggage not tied down should be collected by crew members of other boats.

Putting in at Banks with no Landing Stage

A further problem is putting in at banks not meant for this purpose by leisure craft and rowboats. Suitable places to put in at are flat, sandy banks, approached against the current. The crew should get out when the water is knee-deep, unload the boat and only then pull it out of the water. For a longer break, it is advisable to pull the boat right up onto the shore and store it keel down on a patch of grass.

Putting in at vertical harbour walls is dangerous for crew and equipment as these make getting out and pulling the boat out of the water more difficult. It takes experience and practice to make a rowing excursion in all sorts of conditions possible, e.g. rowing in waters with a strong current, putting in at banks of various forms or inching one's way in very shallow, windy or narrow rivers. A sense of adventure also plays a big role, along with the necessary physical build, skill and psychological toughness.

4. Respect for Nature

The Ten Commandments for Rowers When Dealing With Nature

Every rower should help to protect and support fauna and flora in rivers, lakes and wetlands. Far too many species of plants and animals are in danger of becoming extinct.

1. Avoid pulling in at reedy areas, bullrushes and all other sections of the bank covered in thick and dense plant life. Gravelly, sandy and muddy banks should also be avoided (these are resting and gathering places for birds) as well as thickets on the bank: avoid also shallow waters (spawning areas for fish), especially those with plant life.

2. Maintain a sufficient minimum distance from reeds, bullrushes and other difficult-to-see-through areas of the bank, as well as thickets – on wide rivers at least between 30 m to 50 m. Maintain a sufficient minimum distance from groups of birds on the water – if possible, over 100 metres.

3. Keep strictly to the rules. Watersports are either frequently banned all year round in nature reserves, or at least completely banned for part of the year or only possible under special conditions.

4. Show particular consideration in protected wetlands. These areas serve as biotopes for rare fauna and flora and are hence particularly worthy of protection.

5. When landing, use only those places meant for this purpose or at places where no visible damage can be caused in the process.

6. When on land, do not go near areas of reeds or other such thick vegetation on the bank in order not to invade or endanger the habitats of birds, fish, plants or small animals.

7. When rowing in coastal areas, do not approach seal colonies on the mudflats, so as not to scare them off. Keep at least 300 to 500 m away from where seals are lying or where birds have gathered and at all costs stay close to designated sailing areas. Sail more slowly here.

8. If possible, observe and photograph animals only from a distance.

9. Help keep the water clean. Refuse, especially the contents of chemical toilets should not be disposed of in the water. This matter, just like used oil, must be dispensed of at existing collection points at a harbour area. When in a harbour area, use the sanitary facilities there.

10. Make these rules your own personal ones, and before starting out on a trip, find out the rules for the area you intend to be sailing in. Make sure you pass on this knowledge and your own exemplary behaviour in respect of the environment to young people and especially to those who do not belong to a club.

5. A Few Tips on Staying Healthy during a Rowing Trip

It goes without saying that the following tips apply to both ordinary rowing and competition rowing. The injuries and damage referred to here are only those related to rowing.

Complete information on "First Aid for Sports Injuries" and suggestions for a travelling first aid kit can be found in the handbook for leisure rowers of your national or regional rowing association.

The Contents of a Travelling First Aid Kit

- Sticking plaster for wounds, elastic bandages (6 cm and 8 cm), sticking plastera triangular bandage, surgical gauze (two or three), safety pins, liquid skin disinfectant.
- Sports lotion, ointment for insectbites, vaseline, a lotion and a powder for wounds, deer-tallow (to prevent blisters on the hands).
- Scissors, tweezers, sterile needles.
- Paper handkerchiefs, thermometer.

Protection in Extreme Weather Conditions

Extreme Heat and Sun Exposure

- Wear some form of head-covering, a white, long-sleeved shirt and long pants (this may be a pair of long underpants)
- Apply a sunscreen with a high protection factor (at least factor 6, similar to that worn in the mountains and on the skislopes)
- Drink lots of liquids (mineral water and tea; no alcohol!)
- Cool your whole body or limbs off in the water now and then.

Extreme Cold

Besides a head-covering (ski-cap) and a life jacket, the rower should wear a scarf or something similar to protect his/her neck. Keep the back, particularly the kidney area, especially warm with a long cotton t-shirt. Wear a padded shirt in ice-cold wind.

Heavy Rain

Protect your head, neck and back. If completely wet through, wring out your clothing and put it back on. Put on dry clothing only when your are on land again. Even better: put in and wait for the rain to stop.

Rowing in Winter

In winter both the air and the water can be very cold. When rowing in winter at very low temperatures, the following rules – apart from recommendations on clothing – should be adhered to:

- Never row alone: if possible, row only with a group; beginners should only row with a coach escorting them in a motor boat
- If possible, only row in the vicinity of a bank, so that you can get back onto land quickly if the boat tips over

Injury	Remedies	Preventive Measures
Blisters (on hands and feet)	Only open blood-blisters with a sterile needle, dab dry with a paper handkerchief, apply liquid skin disinfectant, also wound- powder if necessary, then apply a bandage	Row more often to prepare for the trip Deer-tallow, tape up (holds only for a short time)
Raw skin due to rowing	Clean, then apply powder and ointment	Wear well-fitting clothing, no sweaty clothing (gets too salty), fresh, clean clothing
Insect stings	Cool; rub in medication to counter the effects	
Lacerations and scrapes	*Small wounds*: Stop the bleeding, dab dry, disinfect the wound, apply a sticking plaster *Large wounds*: Apply pressure bandage, find a doctor, do not wash with water!	Tetanus injection
Heat stroke, fainting	Put the legs up, bring the patient into the shade, cool down. In case of continuing unconsciousness seek the help of a doctor	Sun-protection, drink liquids, stay out of the heat
Cramps in the calves	Stretch the muscles passively, then relax them, massage gently	Drink liquids (mineral water, electrolytes), if necessary, check the adjustments on the boat

Injury	Remedies	Preventive Measures
Exposure	Warm up quickly in a bathtub; in less serious cases have a long shower. Do not drink any alcohol!	
Boils	Do not touch the boil, apply a bandage after coating the underside with boric acid ointment	Wear clean clothing
Wood splinters in the skin	Remove the visible parts with pincers, apply a bandage; if the splinter is large, seek a doctor's advice	Tetanus injection

Table 26: Treating and avoiding injuries

Basic Training

1. General Principles of Basic Rowing Training

Basic training refers to a certain period of the whole training process. In rowing, it covers the 14–18 year age group. Basic rowing training has the following in common with general fitness training:

- The many and varied demands on movement and loading.

- Year-round practice with seasonal emphasis.

- A small degree of periodised sporting performance and exertion.

Basic training differs from general fitness training in that the former

- is of a limited period and in rowing only lasts about four to five years.

- pursues and aids high-performance goals.

- attempts to align psychological and physical achievements as well as technical and tactical skills in the high-performance area.

- uses competitions to check and gather competition experience .

Basic training is thus a part of the total training process, but is to a large extent a deciding factor in the likelihood of success in high-performance sport.

The following overview puts basic training in its proper place in the overall training process and is supposed to serve as an aid to making long-term plans. The training figures (e.g. times, distances in km, the number of regattas and the number of training units) should be regarded as guidelines only.

Not included in the training figures are the non-standard training measures such as training camps during the holidays or important competitions (see tables 27–29).

Systematic Training Plan for Rowing				
Age	9	10	11	12	13
Training age	–	–	–	–	–
TU/Wk (training units per week)	1–2		2–3		3
Category (age based)		Childrens' rowing			
TU/wk on land in summer in winter				2 1	
TU/Wk in boat in summer in winter				2 1	
Km/yr (km's rowed per year)		500–600		700–800	
No. of regattas/yr	4–6 races 2–3 trips				
No. of races/yr	–	–	–	–	–
Km/TU				6–8	8–10	
Duration/wk (in hrs)	2	3	3.5		4

Table 27: Basic motor training

Particular features of childrens' rowing are:

- Avoidance of overly specialised training. While this may lead to a sharp rise in performance, it also leads to premature stagnation in performance. Various exercises in the neurolocomotor and fitness areas should be set.

- Few training sessions (max. three times a week)

Systematic Training Plan for Rowing					
Age	14	15	16	17	18
Training age	1	2	3	4	5
TU/wk (training units/week)	4	4-6		5-6	6-7
Category (age based)			Junior B		Junior A
TU/wk on land: in summer	1	2		4	
in winter	3	4		2	
TU/wk in boat: in summer	3	4		2	
in winter	1	2		5	
Km/yr (km's rowed per year)	1000	1500		2300	2800
No. of regattas/yr	6	6		7	8
No. of races/yr		20		25	30
Km/TU		10-12		12-15	15-18
Duration/wk in hrs	5-6	6-7		7	10-12

Table 28: Basic training

Systematic Training Plan for Rowing								
Age	19	20	21	22	23	24	25	26
Training age	6	7	8	9	10	11	12	13
TU/wk (training units/week)		6-8		7-9		9-12		
Category (age-based)		Senior B				Senior A		
TU/wk on land: in summer in winter		2 4		3 4		2-3 5		
TU/wk in boat: in summer in winter		6 2		6-8 3-4		9-10 4-5		
Km/yr (km's rowed per year)		3,200	3,500			4,500		
No. of regattas/yr		8-10		8-10		8-10		
No. of races/yr		25-30		30-35		30 +		
Km/TU		6-20		18-20		20 +		
Duration/wk in hrs		2-15		15-18		18 +		

Table 29: High-performance training

- Not too many competitions.
- Coach should become a role model and encourage the children to be independent.
- Create opportunities for other leisure opportunities outside the club.

Basic rowing training is preceded by *general motor training*, which must be partly covered by school sports and partly by club sports. Sports offering exercise in the general movement and exertion area – appropriate to children's physical and intellectual development – stretching the body in many ways form a good basis for this.

Basic training is not a rigid plan for the period mentioned. It lies in a continuum between general elementary motor training and specialised high-performance training. During this period, the exercises change from being of a general and specific nature to those with a high rowing-related content performed on the water.

Exercises Promoting General Physical Development

The extent to which a physical exercise or training-related exertion can be categorised as *promoting general physical development* depends on the type of sport being engaged in. For rowers, games, various forms of light athletics, and gymnastics all promote general physical development, but have nothing or little in common with the exertion or movements in rowing.

Yet this sort of highly developed general motor training forms an excellent basis for developing specific abilities for rowing. In addition, a high standard in this area improves the ability to recover from loads and reduces the likelihood of injuries.

Specialised Exercises

Exercises are *specialised* when they show typically rowing-related characteristics such as endurance and strength endurance, as well as the movement-related and dynamic coordination movement sequences in rowing. Here, exercises on strength training apparatuses should be mentioned first. When broken down into part movements, these show natural movements similar to those used in rowing: rowing machine, bench presses, leg exercises, weightlifting, etc.

But even exercises and sports guaranteeing a high degree of transferability to rowing such as aerobic endurance in skiing, cycling or running can also be regarded as specialised exercises in basic training.

Competition Exercises

This means performing the sport of rowing itself. Competition exercises should not be confused with training specifically for competitions, which means training at competition speed (or just over or under this speed) in particular.

The breakdown for rowing in terms of the intended training effect takes place with the help of the categories of exertion and areas of intensity. Whether an exercise is of *general nature*, a *special* or a *competition exercise* depends on how far it can be transferred to the sporting aim, for example, a rowing race over a length of 2,000 m. Even this breakdown is very analytical. One must imagine a continuum applied to the types of sports, forms of training and training equipment having regard to the required movement and exertion as well as the development of the individual rower.

In general, the following principle applies:
• the lower the training age
• the lower the biological age of the rower
• the worse the level of performance
• the further off important races are

the more important the fundamentals are and the greater the amount of *general physical exercises* needs to be.

Conversely the following principle also applies:
• the higher the training age,
• the higher the performance level,
• the nearer important races move,
• the better the rowing technique,

the greater the exertion in special areas of training or in the boat must be. The development of special training equipment in high-performance rowing (ergometer, windwheel or strength training equipment) makes this requirement clear.

While the ratio between general and special forms of training on the one hand and competition training on the other hand is about 60:40 during basic training, towards the end, it is about 45:55. At the beginning of top rowing it is about 40:60 and at the extreme it is about 25:75 (see figure 21).

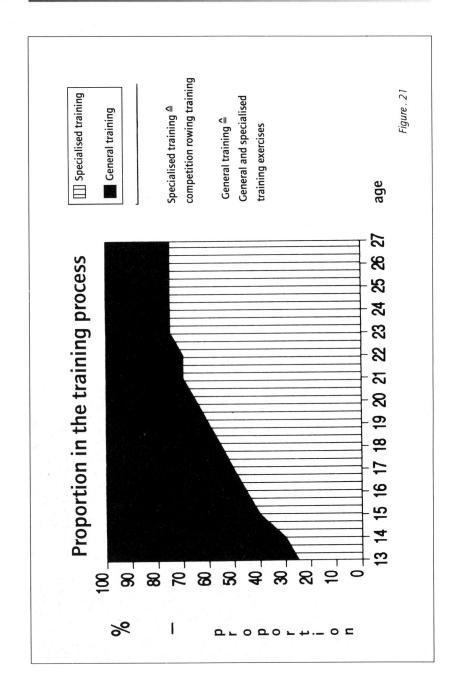

Figure. 21

2. Planning Basic Training

Annual Training Plan

The following overview gives tips as to how to design a training plan using the example of a third-year Junior B rower. The ratio of general and specific training to competition training is about 55:45. *General fitness training* during the course of the year and limiting training to a maximum of six training units per week, is considered important. The degree of exertion in individual training units is not prescribed in detail; it lies between:

- in basic endurance between category V-IV
- in rowing "technique" (RT) in category VI
- on rowing endurance (extensive) in category V
- in rowing endurance (intensive) in category IV
- in rowing strength endurance (RPS) in category III
- in competition rowing in category II und I
- in power training it is based on general strength.

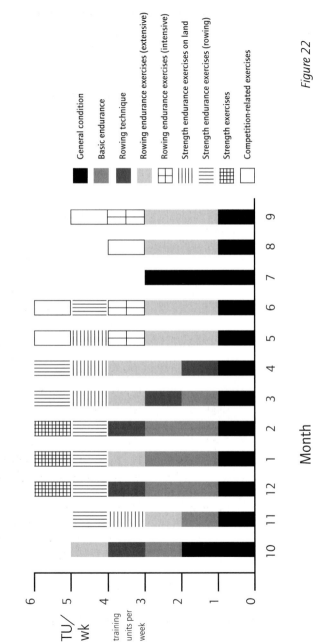

Figure 22

Weekday	Training	
Monday	Goal:	general fitness
	Duration:	about 70–80 min
	Exertion:	high
	Content:	gymnastics, strengthening with a medicine ball, strength endurance with a partner, game (hockey), intensive endurance exercises
Tuesday	free (school sport?)	
Wednesday	Goal:	general & specialised strength endurance
	Duration:	about 60–70 min
	Exertion:	very high
	Content:	warm-up, gymnastics, circuit training: 8 stations, 3 rounds, 25–30 repetitions per exercise, about 600 repetitions in all
Thursday	Goal:	improving rowing technique
	Duration:	60–70 min
	Exertion:	negligible
	Content:	rowing exercises to improve team coordination, endurance (category VI)
Friday	Goal:	basic endurance
	Duration:	45 min
	Exertion:	average
	Content:	cross-country run (category V)
Saturday	Goal:	rowing-related strength endurance
	Duration:	70 min
	Exertion:	high
	Content:	15 min rowing to warm up at an SR of 18–20 then two full-power pieces at 20, 30 and 40 strokes 2–3 min break (category V)
Sunday	free	

Table 30: An example of a weekly training plan (November) for a Junior B rower, aged 16 in the 3rd year of training

Weekday		Training
Monday	Goal: Duration: Exertion: Content:	general fitness 60 min neglible stretching gymnastics, flexibility, games, aerobic endurance exercises
Tuesday	free (school sport?)	
Wednesday	Goal: Duration: Exertion: Content:	rowing-related power endurance, intensive endurance 70–80 min high rowing (category III-IV)
Thursday	Goal: Duration: Exertion: Content:	technique training, aerobic endurance 60 min neglible-to-average exercises to improve putting oars in the water & taking them out again endurance (category VI-V)
Friday	Goal: Duration: Exertion: Content:	intensive endurance exercises 70–80 min high rowing (category IV)
Saturday	Goal: Duration: Exertion: Content:	aerobic endurance exercises 70 min average rowing (category V), ten racing strokes every five minutes
Sunday	Goal: Duration: Exertion: Content:	competition-related endurance exercises starts and spurts 70 min high loosening up by rowing, 15 minute warm-up, 2 x 20 stroke starts, 1 x 500 m at racing pace (SS), 1 x 1000 m SF at racing pace (ss 2), 1 x 20 strokes from a standing start, winding down (category I, III)

Weekday		Training
Monday	Goal: Duration: Exertion: Content:	recovery, aerobic endurance 60 min neglible rowing followed by a run (category VI)
Tuesday	Goal: Duration: Exertion: Content:	general fitness 60 min neglible-to-average gymnastics, exercises in flexibility, games
Wednesday	Goal: Duration: Exertion: Content:	intensive endurance 70–80 min high 15 min rowing to warm up, (category V), 1 x 6 min piece (category IV), 2 x 3 min piece (category III), 1 x 6 min piece (category VI), 5 min break, winding down for 30 min (category VI)
Thursday	Goal: Duration: Exertion: Content:	recovery, aerobic endurance, tactics 60 min neglible-to-average 20 min rowing (category V), practising starts up to a maximum of 10 strokes/min, 1 x 20 stroke start, 20 min rowing to wind down (category VI)
Friday	free	
Saturday	Regatta: Exertion:	1–2 races high to very high (category II)
Sunday	Regatta: Exertion:	1–2 races high to very-high (category III)

Table 31: Example of a 2-week training plan in June

PART 4: APPENDIX

The Most Important Competition Rules

The *"Code des Courses"* (Racing Code, or CdC) of the *"Fédération Internationale des Sociétés d'Aviron"* (*International Federation of Rowing Clubs*, under the auspices of FISA) and the *"Reglement des Championats"* govern international regattas. The rules are subject to alteration and adjustment by the Rowing Conference, which usually takes place every two years. The following are the most important current competition rules of the *German Rowing Association* (most of these are FISA rules as well):

1. Age-groups
2. Course lengths
3. Weight regulations for Lightweights
4. Categories of boats for championship races

1. Age groups

Junior B's (Boys and Girls)
who have turned 15 or 16 by December 31st.

Junior A's (Men and Women)
who have turned 17 or 18 by December 31st.

Mens' and Womens' B
who have turned 19, 20, 21 or 22 by December 31st.

Mens' and Womens' A
who are neither Juniors nor belong to the B Group.

Children
those children who have turned 14 by December 31st are entitled to take part.

Men and women 27 years of age and over (Masters)

A Minimum age: 27
B Minimum average age: 36
C Minimum average age: 43
D Minimum average age: 50
E Minimum average age: 55
F Minimum age: 60
G Minimum age: 65
H Minimum age: 70

The last day to qualify for any given age group is December 31st of the rowing year.

2. Course Lengths

Normal racing length courses (in racing boats)

Men, Women and Junior A's	2000 m
Junior B's	1500 m
Men and Women 27 years and over (Masters)	1000 m

In a tub   1000 m +

Long-distance races ("Heads")   minimum 4000 m

Sprints   about 500 m

3. Weight Regulations for Lightweights (in kg)

	Men	Junior Men A	B	Women	Junior Women A	B
Team Individ.	70	65	62.5	57	55	52.5
Weight Single	72.5	67.5	65	59	57.5	55
Scullers	72.5	65	62.5	57	55	52.5

4. Categories of Boats for Championship Races

Category	Men	Women	Junior A Men	Junior A Women
Single scull				
Double scull				
Quadruple scull (Quad)				
(Coxless) pair				
Coxed pair				
Coxless four				
Coxed four				
Eight				

These boats are used for open and lightweight events.

These boats are used only for open events.

Not used in this category.

Please order our catalogue!

Our Programme

Jozef Sneyers
Soccer Training ●
An Annual Programme

ISBN 1-84126-017-7
c. DM 34 ,-/SFr 31,60/ÖS 248,-
£ 12.95/US$ 19.95
Austr.$ 29.95/Can$ 29.95

Gerhard Frank
Soccer Training Programmes

ISBN 3-89124-556-4
DM 29,80/SFr 27,70/ÖS 218,-
£ 12.95/US$ 17.95
Austr.$ 29.95/Can$ 25.95

Ilona E. Gerling
Teaching Children's Gymnastics

ISBN 3-89124-549-1
DM 29,80/SFr 27,70/ÖS 218,-
£ 12.95/US $ 17.95
Austr.$ 29.95/Can$ 25.95

Bischops/Gerards
Soccer
Warming-up and Cooling down

ISBN 1-84126-014-2
c. DM 24,80/SFr 23,-/ÖS 181,-
£ 8.95/US$ 14.95
Austr.$24.95/Can$ 20.95

Bischops/Gerards
Junior Soccer:
A Manual for Coaches

ISBN 1-84126-000-2
DM 29,80/SFr 27,70/ÖS 218,-
£ 12.95/US$ 17.95
Austr.$ 29.95/Can$ 25.95

Thomas Kaltenbrunner
Contact Improvisation

ISBN 3-89124-485-1
DM 29,80/SFr 27,70/ÖS 218,-
£ 12.95/US$ 17.95
Austr.$ 29.95/Can$ 25.95

Bischops/Gerards
Soccer ●
One-On-One

ISBN 1-84126-013-4
c. DM 24,80/SFr 23,-/ÖS 181,-
£ 8.95/US$ 14.95
Austr.$24.95/Can$ 20.95

Bischops/Gerards
Coaching Tips for Children's Soccer

ISBN 3-89124-529-7
DM 14,80/SFr 14,40/ÖS 108,-
£ 5.95/US$ 8.95
Austr.$ 14.95/Can$ 12.95

Dörte Wessel-Therhorn
Jazz Dance Training

ISBN 3-89124-499-1
DM 29,80/SFr 27,70/ÖS 218,-
£ 12.95/US$ 17.95
Austr.$ 29.95/Can$ 25.95

Gerhard Frank
Soccer ●
Creative Training

ISBN 1-84126-015-0
c. DM 24,80/SFr 23,-/ÖS 181,-
£ 8.95/US$ 14.95
Austr.$24.95/Can$ 20.95

Pieter/Heijmans
Scientific Coaching for Olympic Taekwondo

ISBN 3-89124-389-8
DM 29,80/SFr 27,70/ÖS 218,-
£ 12.95/US$ 17.95
Austr.$ 29.95/Can$ 25.95

Bergmann/Butz
Adventure Sports – Big Foot

ISBN 3-89124-497-5
DM 34 ,-/SFr 31,60/ÖS 248,-
£ 14.95/US$ 19.95
Austr.$ 29.95/Can$ 29.95

Erich Kollath
Soccer ●
Techniques & Tactics

ISBN 1-84126-016-9
c. DM 24,80/SFr 23,-/ÖS 181,-
£ 8.95/US$ 14.95
Austr.$24.95/Can$ 20.95

Rudolf Jakhel
Modern Sports Karate

ISBN 3-89124-428-2
DM 29,80/SFr 27,70/ ÖS 218,-
£ 12.95/US$ 17.95
Austr.$ 29.95/Can$ 25.95

Münch/ Mund
Straight Golf

ISBN 3-89124-503-3
DM 34,-/SFr 31,60/ÖS 248,-
£ 12.95/US$ 19.95
Austr.$ 29.95/Can$ 25.95

● In preparation

MEYER
&MEYER
SPORT

Our Programme

MEYER & MEYER SPORT

Meyer & Meyer Sport • Von-Coels-Str. 390 • D-52080 Aachen • Fax: 0049241/9 58 10 10

e-mail: verlag@meyer-meyer-sports.com • **Please order by:** www.meyer-meyer-sports.com

Our Programme

Gudrun Paul
Aerobic Training ●

ISBN 1-84126-021-5
DM 29,80/SFr 27,70/ÖS 218,-
£ 12.95/US$ 17.95
Austr.$ 29.95/Can$ 25.95

Unger/Rössler
Bodywork – Power for Women ●

ISBN 1-84126-022-3
DM 29,80/SFr 27,70/ÖS 218,-
£ 12.95/US$ 17.95
Austr.$ 29.95/Can$ 25.95

Diel/Menges
Surfing ●
In search of the perfect wave

ISBN 1-84126-023-1
DM 29.80/SFr 27,70/ÖS 218,-
£ 12.95/US $ 17.95
Austr. $ 29.95/Can $ 25.95

Wolfgang Fritsch
Rowing ●

ISBN 1-84126-024-X
DM 34 ,-/SFr 31,60/ÖS 248,-
£ 14.95/US$ 19.95
Austr.$ 29.95/Can$ 29.95

Green/Hardman (eds.)
Physical Education A Reader

ISBN 3-89124-463-0
DM 39,80/SFr 37,-/ÖS 291,-
£ 17.95/US $ 29,-
Austr.$ 37.95/ Can$ 39.95

Arthur Lydiard revolutionised the training of middle and long distance runners in the 1960s. Since then his methods have contributed to the success of countless athletes around the world, including four time Olympic gold medalist and world record setter Lasse Viren of Finland.

Lydiard/Gilmour
Distance Training for Women Athletes

ISBN 1-84126-002-9
DM 24,80/SFr 23,-/ÖS 181,-
£ 9.95/US$ 14.95
Austr.$ 24.95/Can$ 20.95

Lydiard/Gilmour
Distance Training for Young Athletes

ISBN 3-89124-533-5
DM 29,80/SFr 27,70/ÖS 218,-
£ 12.95/US$ 17.95
Austr.$ 29.95/Can$ 25.95

Lydiard Gilmour
Distance Training for Masters

ISBN 1-84126-018-5
c. DM 29,80/SFr 27,70/ÖS 218,-
£ 12.95/US$ 17.95
Austr.$ 29.95/Can$ 25.95

Arthur Lydiard
Running to the Top

ISBN 3-89124-440-1
DM 29,80/SFr 27,70/ÖS 218,-
£ 12.95/US$ 17.95
Austr.$ 29.95/Can$ 25.95

Do you want to improve your training? – Let Lydiard be your personal coach!
For US$ 240,-/year only Lydiard offers you personal training plans and advice.

For more information turn to

www.lydiard.com

or

www.meyer-meyer-sports.com

MEYER
&MEYER
SPORT